# NEW
# STEPS

## PAUL GROVES · JOHN GRIFFIN

NATIONAL CURRICULUM · KEY STAGE 3

# BOOK 2

# THE NATIONAL WHAT?

A pupil's guide to the National Curriculum in English.

## What is the National Curriculum?

If you looked up the words in a dictionary you would find:

*national* (a) public, general, applying to one's country.

*curriculum* (n) a course of study.

So the National Curriculum is a course of study that is nation-wide – what every pupil in Britain should try to know and be able to do.

## How does it work?

What sorts of skills would you most likely be learning in English?

English is about communication between people, whether you are reading your favourite author or explaining your illness to your doctor. A simple task such as this needs all the main English skills. To visit your doctor you might need to READ a bus timetable, the destination of the bus, the name of the road where the surgery is. Fortunately the chemist has to read the doctor's HANDWRITING, but you will certainly need your skills of SPEAKING and LISTENING to explain what is wrong and listen to the doctor's advice. You'll need to fill in a form at the surgery (READING, UNDERSTANDING and WRITING) which

won't please the receptionist if it's untidy and full of crossings out (PRESENTATION) and inaccurate words (SPELLING).

So the National Curriculum for English will help you to improve in these areas; READING, SPEAKING and LISTENING, WRITING, SPELLING, HANDWRITING and PRESENTATION

## I'm doing all those already.

Yes, and that's one of several reasons why you shouldn't worry about the National Curriculum. But you can improve all of them, can't you?

## Well, I'd do that without the National Curriculum so what's new?

Have you made a radio play, written a story for young children, made a teenage magazine? Can you fill in a form as well as you can write a story, made an advert as well as you can write a business letter? Do you change what you say and how you say it according to your audience? Do you know what Standard English is? Are you interested in dialect and accent? Can you always find what you're looking for in your library? Do you always know what you are looking for? Do you know what present tense means, or narrative poem?

## It's a poem that tells a story.

Ah, well you had us there. Good. But we've given you some idea of the range you'll cover. One of the big differences is that SPEAKING and LISTENING will count as much as READING or WRITING.

## Count for what?

When you're assessed.

*You mean tested. I thought you'd come to that.*

It's not too bad, really. You are following the Programmes of Study, the kinds of things we've mentioned, and your teacher will keep some record of how you're progressing in the Attainment Targets – they're just checks that you've covered all the material. There are Attainment Targets for each of the five areas of English and you could progress up them from Level 1 to Level 10.

*That sounds very hard. I don't think I'll bother with it.*

You have to; it's the Law. And it's not as complicated as it sounds. You've probably reached Level 5 for each of the targets already. You're on Stage 3 (one of the four Key Stages in your learning) which lasts until you're fourteen.

*I'm not happy about these Attainment Targets.*

Well, let's take one of them as an example, a general one that covers much of your work: 'Pupils should be able to recognise and respond to a variety of forms and styles of writing.'

*You see. That still sounds hard.*

Look at these pieces from this book:

1 NARRATOR: Sh . . . stop again. I can hear something else. What is it this time?
 FX (SOUND EFFECTS): Footsteps stop. Cowshed door opens. Mooing cows.

2 I shall not be listening to any more of these ridiculous stories.
   Yours faithfully,
   L. W. Morton

3 The king sacrificed before the God and when night came he was taken into the temple.

4 He'd hardly gone, when there were a knockin' agen the winder. She upped and opened it and there were the little owd thing.

5 HUNTSMAN SHOT DEAD BY HIS DOG

6 Break seal with a sharp knife.

Now if you can say which is part of a letter, which is an instruction, a newspaper headline, a play for younger children, a story in dialect, a myth, you will show you've already learned much about different ways of writing.
The point we're making is that you can already do many of the things in the National Curriculum.

*How will I prove it?*

All the time – in your normal work. When you're at the end of the stage you're on (it's all Key Stage 3) there will be tests to see how you've done.

*What! Tests! What tests?*

There are tests at 7, 11, 14 and 16. So you've missed two already. They're national tests; so everybody does them. And they will be just the kind of work you've been doing. You might make a poetry anthology, a magazine, some project like that – nothing very headbreaking, and probably enjoyable. They are checks on your ability in the Attainment Targets for READING, WRITING, SPEAKING and LISTENING.

*Maybe it will be O.K.*

Try the book; see how you get on!

# Contents

**1 A radio play for young children**    8

Know your audience    8
The Scarecrow    9
A letter about the play    13
A performance    14
Make the play into a story    14
Write your own radio play    15

**2 Pamphlets and instructions**    18

How does a pamphlet work?    18
Write a summary    18
The pamphlet's purpose    21
Make your own pamphlet    21
Mr Willow teaches the exclamation mark!    22
Now listen carefully!    23
Verbal instructions    26

**3 Using the dictionary**    27

Make the dictionary your friend    27
Alphabetical order    28
What words mean    28
Parts of speech    28

**4 Verb power and sentences**    31

Working with words    31
Re-cap: parts of speech you already know    32
Learning to use sentences    33
So what happened?    33
Make startling sentences    34
Ernulf's long sentence    35
Spot the sentence    36

**5 Stories from the past**    37

Myths and legends    37
The Children of the Cloud    38
Continue the myth    44

**6  Ghostly happenings**                                        45

Be a reporter                                                    45
Write a summary                                                  45
Write a ghost story                                              45
Role play 1                                                      48
Role play 2                                                      48


**7  The power of the verb**                                     49

The making of a sentence                                         49
Verbs control what happens                                       50
Change the tense                                                 50
Choose the verb                                                  50
Mr Willow teaches the comma                                      53


**8  Dialect and Standard English**                              55

A dialect fairy tale                                             55
Tom Tit Tot                                                      55
Received pronunciation                                           61
Your own local story                                             61
Agreement – the subject and the verb                             61
Singular and plural with the verb 'to be'                        61
Finding the subject                                              62
Singular and plural with the present tense                       62


**9  Play making**                                               64

Help in writing your plays                                       64
Putting in the words                                             66
What shall I write a play about?                                 66
Cliff-hangers                                                    67
Language in plays                                                69
Plays to complete                                                70

**10   Arguing it out**                                                73

    Arguing logically                                74
    Write a summary                                  74
    Do you agree?                                    74
    Children's rights societies                      76

**11   Letters**                                                       77

    Get the content and style right                  77
    Business letters                                 79

**12   Improving your writing**                                        82

    Looking at a famous poem                         82
    The Rime of the Ancient Mariner   *Samuel Taylor Coleridge*   83
    Complete the tale                                86
    Similes                                          86
    Clichés                                          87

**13   The world of advertising**                                      91

    Images                                           91
    Write your own advertising copy                  92

**14   Things that happen in real life**                               96

    The Visitor   *H. Orlando Patterson*             97
    Equal Rights   *Bernard Ashley*                  100
    Write your own story                             104
    Write a book review                              104
    Conversation: direct speech                      105

**15   You and your library**                                          106

    Understanding a book's number                    106
    Making groups                                    107
    How a subject gets its number                    108
    Finding a non-fiction book                       109
    Making notes                                     110

**16  Make your own magazine**                                           112

A longer project                                                          112
The comic                                                                 114
An argument                                                               115
A serial story                                                            117
The unusual                                                               118
A quiz                                                                    119
The problem page                                                          120
The feature article                                                       120
The book review                                                           122
Get your story                                                            123

# A RADIO PLAY FOR YOUNG CHILDREN

## 1

In this Step we want you to think of the audience you are writing for in each task you do. You will be asked to write for young children.
We also want you to get used to assessing your own work.
The Step ends with your old friend the Spell Well.

## Know your audience

'Now, my dear, shall I see if I can find you a sweetie and a comic?'
'No thanks, I'll just have a whisky and the *Times* crossword.'

Before you speak or write, ask yourself:

What words are best suited to express my purpose to this particular *audience*?

Read the script on pages 9–12.

# The Scarecrow

TAPE    Opening signal

FX    Country farm atmosphere (WINTER). Distant rooks

NARRATOR    Hello . . . Have you ever been to the country? If so, perhaps you've seen me out in the fields. My head's a big, green turnip and my nose is a long, orange carrot. I'm wearing an old jacket and scruffy, checked trousers stuffed with straw and tied up with string. Oops . . . and there's something tickling and wriggling under my hat.

FX    Rustle of straw. Field mouse squeaking

NARRATOR    Why, it's a little field mouse. She's making a cosy nest in my long straw hair.
Have you guessed what I am? I'm a . . . scarecrow.
My name's Barley-Jo.

Before I start our story today, take turns to say what you think we scarecrows are like, and if you know what we're used for, tell everyone about that too.

TAPE  Signal (pause)

FX  Country atmosphere

NARRATOR  We scarecrows have a very important job to do. Farmers put us in their fields to frighten away the birds and stop them eating the crops they've planted.
But sometimes I get bored in my big, ploughed field. It gets very lonely with only the mice and the wind for company.
But today is special. It's the day of the Scarecrows' Barn Dance. You can come with me, but only scarecrows are allowed so first you must dress up like me.
Stand up and go to a space in the field where you can put on your baggy old scarecrow clothes.

FX  Putting on trousers, tying string, shaking jacket and putting it on, putting on hat, stuffing straw in boots, putting boots on: (to run under)

NARRATOR  Big, baggy trousers first . . . wriggle one foot in . . . now the other. Pull them right up to your armpits (pause). Now pick up some string and tie it round your waist tightly, that'll stop your trousers slipping down (pause). Boots next . . . They're much too big to dance in so, before you put them on, stuff some straw in the end to make them fit better . . . first one . . . and now the other. Put them on . . . Do them up . . . if the laces are broken you'll have to use some more string . . . Now your jacket. Give it a big shake to make sure there are no spiders or field mice hiding in it (pause), and slip it on. Do up the buttons . . . one . . . two . . . three (pause).
And now last of all pick up your hat . . . pull it down over your straw hair . . . and tuck a feather or flower in one side, to make it extra smart (pause).
There, you look just like a scarecrow now, but before we go to the barn dance, you'd better practise walking like a scarecrow too, so no one will guess you're a human. Stretch both your elbows out . . . Make your legs very stiff and straight like sticks . . . and let your head go very floppy and wobbly . . . Stay in your scarecrow shape and get ready to take stiff, jerky scarecrow steps across the field, and down to the farm. Ready, come on.

FX  Farmyard atmosphere

NARRATOR  In a moment we'll make our way over to the Big Barn where the Dance is being held. But we'll have to be as quiet as field mice. We don't want the farmer to know we've left his field unguarded. He'll be very angry if he thinks the birds are eating all his crops.

So get ready to do your scarecrow walk over to the barn as quietly as you can. Keep looking and listening all the time. If you hear anyone coming stop walking and stand as still and quiet as a scarecrow in a field until I tell you it's safe to carry on. No talking, not even whispering. Come on, begin to creep across the farmyard with me now.

**FX** <u>Scarecrow walking across a farmyard</u>

| NARRATOR | Take slow, careful steps . . . keep a sharp eye open for the farmer, we don't want him to catch us here . . . and keep listening . . . remember if you hear anyone coming, stand still so no one will notice you . . . |
|---|---|
| FX | Sheep dog running out barking (approaching) |
| NARRATOR | Stop . . . what's that sound? |
| FX | Dog barking closer |
| NARRATOR | Oh, it's alright. It's only Jep the sheepdog. He won't hurt us. Carry on walking slowly across the yard, but keep looking and listening for danger. |
| FX | Scarecrow walking (cont). Approaching footsteps (a person in wellies). Clanking buckets |
| NARRATOR | Ssh . . . stop again. I can hear something else. What is it this time? |
| FX | Footsteps stop. Cow-shed door opens. Mooing cows |
| NARRATOR | We're safe. It's only the farmer's daughter off to feed the cows. We've nearly reached the barn. Creep forward again. |
| FX | Scarecrow walking (cont). Approaching geese. Hissing and flapping wings |
| NARRATOR | Stand still again . . . Do you know what's making that noise? It's the farm geese. They're very bossy and noisy, but they won't hurt us. Anyway, here we are at the barn. Let's open the door and go inside . . . |
| FX | Barn door opens. Barn dance music. |
| NARRATOR | Sit down on the bales of straw . . . Here we are at the Scarecrows' Barn Dance. |

▭ Discuss the following in class:

Is this piece meant to be read, listened to or performed on a stage? Give reasons.
What age group is it for? Give examples from the story-line and the words used to support your answer.
What does FX mean? Can you work out what 'to run under' might mean?
For what purpose is the Tape Signal?

## A letter about the play

Your first long piece of work will be to write a similar play for children. To do this well, you have to be able to enter a child's world. The words you use and the type of story you write have to appeal to children.
Read this (imaginary) letter of complaint.

3 Pastures Way
Blixton
Hampshire
SO33 9NE
August 6th

Dear Sir

I wish to protest most strongly about the scarecrow story you broadcast last Friday.
For a start there was far too much time spent describing the scarecrow and its job. My wife and I listened through it patiently for the story to start, only to discover the scarecrow was going to a barn dance. This is absolute rubbish and you know it. Scarecrows can't dance – or speak, eat or move for that matter.
But worse was to follow. Suddenly we were asked to put on baggy scarecrow clothes. We have some old gardening clothes in a box upstairs, but we were given no chance to fetch them before we were supposed to be walking stiff-legged to the barn dance. I tried pulling my trousers up under my armpits and that didn't do me any good, I can tell you.
I shall not be listening to any of these silly stories again.

Yours faithfully

L.W. Martin

▭ Write a letter of reply. Imagine you are the producer of the series called *Let's Make a Story*. What has L.W. Martin misunderstood about the story 'The Scarecrow'?

*FOOTNOTE*

Note the way the letter is set out. The modern letter requires no **punctuation** in the address and date, the **salutation** (Dear . . .), the **subscription** (Yours . . .) or on the envelope. Your teacher may still believe in using punctuation. If you do use punctuation, use it throughout the letter. Most writers leave out the odd comma or full-stop which is wrong in the address. Note how the letter is in paragraphs. It is essential to **paragraph** a letter as you raise each point.

*FOOTNOTE*

In the play the word *alright* has been used. This will still not be in some dictionaries as the correct spelling is *all right*. However, this is an example of a word in change. The Americans spell it *alright* and television tends to do this too. There is a show called *It'll be alright on the night*.
By the end of the century we expect all people will write *alright* as it makes more sense because we have:

also   already   altogether   always   almost

Note: *a lot* is nothing to do with these. Never write *alot*. It is always two words.

## A performance

⇨ In groups of three, practise (and record on tape if possible) part of the piece. Choose a **narrator**. The other two will need to make the sound effects (FX).

## Make the play into a story

⇨ Write 'The Scarecrow' as a complete story for children (6–7 years old). You will have no sound effects, but you won't be limited to one speaker – the narrator. For instance, the farmer could interrupt the barn dance looking for the missing scarecrow. Does he catch her or does she get back to the field without being noticed? Do other scarecrows or animals come into the story? Which of them talk? When you have finished compare your story with the original. What has been lost or gained?

# Write your own radio play

➡ It is now time to write your own radio play for children. You are meant to involve the children (6–7 year olds) in the performance. These are possible titles:

A visit (museum, zoo, park).
The toybox – toys coming to life at night.
The firefighter – the children are firemen or firewomen.

Study how our radio play was set out and do yours in the same layout.

**Remember that children are much more willing to imagine and take part than adults or teenagers, so give them several things to do.** (The Tape Signal is a pause for activities – to discuss, tell each other, or perform.) Record your finished pieces, if you can.

# ASSESSMENT

Each creative piece of work in this book is prepared for by reading or performing other people's work, by learning the right ways to set out content, and by getting to know any specialised or technical terms needed.

Most of you will be putting completed pieces in a folder. For each one a record sheet would be useful, acting as revision and helping you to make assessments of your performance.

On page 16 there is an example of a Record Sheet that you can adapt to use from time to time throughout the book. Copy it out and complete it for yourself. It will be useful as a revision exercise, a record of what you have learnt and achieved and a way of judging how well you have understood and created (made) similar pieces of your own. Write your Record Sheets in four parts:

1 *Preparation*
   How you prepared, the reading, the searching for information, etc.

2 *Oral*
   An account of any discussions or performances that took place.

3 *Written work*
   What you wrote: details of story-lines, letters, etc.
   Anything you had to re-draft to improve.
   Anything you discovered about writing.

4 *Assessment*
   Your view of how well you did the set task.
   Your friends' views and the group's views.
   Sometimes your teacher's view of how you might have improved it.

— — — — — — — — — — — — — — —

# Record Sheet

## Preparation

1 We read a piece called 'The Scarecrow'. I knew it was a radio play for young children because . . .

Give several reasons, referring to both the story-line and the vocabulary (words used).

2 We replied to a letter of complaint about the programme saying that the story was silly. The points I made in my letter were . . .

Mention in particular the need to have programmes suitable for different types of audience.

## Oral

1 We performed part of 'The Scarecrow'. I was the narrator and I enjoyed this role because . . .

Write a personal account of what happened and how well you thought you and the group performed. What part did you take? How were the parts decided? Did you enjoy it? What mistakes were made?

## Written work

1 We made the play of 'The Scarecrow' into a story for children. I decided to have the animals talk because children . . .

Describe what you did, how you changed the story and any new ideas you invented.
The differences between the radio play and the story were . . .
The advantages of the story version were . . .
The advantages of the radio version were . . .

2 We wrote our own radio play for children. I decided to write about a child's room where at night the toys take charge and the children are played with . . .

Describe what subject you chose, the story-line you followed and the sound effects you used.
Did you have any difficulty in keeping the story and the language simple enough?

## Assessment

1 I got my younger sister and some of her friends to take the parts of the toys. Some of the words were too difficult for them, so I made some changes as we were reading it through . . .

If you used children as performers, describe how this worked. If you performed to a group of your class, describe your own and their reactions. If you tried your play out on a younger brother or sister, say how interested they were. Record the reactions to your play.
How satisfied were you with what you did? Did you make any alterations after you had thought about your work and listened to others' reactions?

# SPELL WELL

To help you with your spelling, we want you to add to the word families where you see the Spell Well sign in this book.

cookery forsook booking rookery

With this group you can make:

paid maid said unaided plaid

Can you think of any others?
Keep your own dictionary, a page for each letter of the alphabet. Choose the two words you might find the most difficult to spell from each family and put them in your dictionary, for example, plaid, unaided.
Here are two to pick from:

thought sought bought drought

# PAMPHLETS AND INSTRUCTIONS

## 2

Writing is not just for entertainment, like a radio play. Writing can be for serious purposes like saving lives. More and more pamphlets are being issued to help you have a full and healthy life. We include one of them in this Step.

We also take a fun look at the exclamation mark when you will meet a formidable teacher called Mr Willow.

Finally, can you give instructions? We give you some oral practice.

## How does a pamphlet work?

Study the pamphlet *HOW TO TAKE YOUR MEDICINE* on pages 19–20.

### Write a summary

⇨ Imagine you have been asked to make a **summary** (a shorter form) of the pamphlet. Write down the five points you think are most important and summarise them in a single paragraph beginning:

'The pamphlet gives general advice about taking medicine. It emphasises that you should . . .'

⇨ Discuss the pamphlet in class. Decide if there are any points that are so obvious they don't need mentioning. What use does the pamphlet make of illustration, *capitals*, short sentences, short paragraphs, different sized type, *italics*, *sub-headings*? Are all the illustrations

# HOW TO TAKE YOUR MEDICINE

a message from your Pharmacist

Read the label on your medicine carefully. It tells you WHO should take it; HOW MUCH to take; WHEN to take it; and HOW to take it.

## Who should take the medicine?

Only the person whose name is on the label should take it. No-one else should, even if they seem to have the same illness.

## How much medicine to take

Only take the amount shown on the label. Taking more medicine will not make it work faster or better and it could harm you. If in doubt ask your pharmacist.

Make sure that if the medicine is for a child, the doctor knows the child's age. If not, tell the pharmacist. This is important.

## When to take the medicine

Medicines act in different ways. Some begin to work in the mouth before being swallowed. Some are absorbed in the stomach, others in the intestine. So if the label says take the medicine *before food* it means on an empty stomach; *after food* means when you have eaten a meal. If it says *just before going to bed* there is an important reason for that. Follow the instructions carefully.

## Be Careful!

Some medicines have special instructions as well. Follow them all, especially warnings such as **'Avoid alcoholic drink'** or **'Do not drive or operate machinery'**. Alcohol or other medicines may change the way your medicine works. You may be told **'Do not drive'** because your medicine may make you sleepy or dizzy.

The label may say **'Complete the prescribed course unless otherwise directed'**. This means you should finish the medicine even if you begin to feel well. If you don't finish all the medicine, some germs may not be killed and you may become ill again.

If you are taking other medicines at the same time you should tell your doctor. If you forget, ask the pharmacist if they are safe to take together. This is very important because one medicine could affect the others.

Don't keep old medicines in your home. Flush them down the toilet, or ask the pharmacist to destroy them for you.

## How to take the medicine

Make sure you know how to take your medicines.

Tablets and capsules can stick in your throat so take them with plenty of water while sitting or standing up.

If your medicine is in *capsules*, swallow them whole unless you are told to open them up.

If the medicine is liquid and the pharmacist gives you a special 5ml spoon — use it because that will make it easier to measure the correct amount.

# Keep all medicines out of the reach of children

# HOW TO TAKE YOUR MEDICINE

## a message from your Pharmacist

### What to remember in a Pharmacy

## Don't feel well?

If you don't feel well, but don't think you need to go to your doctor, this is what you should do:

- ☐ Ask to speak personally to your pharmacist.
- ☐ Describe what is wrong with you. The pharmacist may suggest that you should go to your doctor — you should follow the pharmacist's advice.
- ☐ Mention any medicines you are already taking.
- ☐ Tell your pharmacist if you are sensitive or allergic to aspirin or any other medicines.
- ☐ If the advice is not for yourself, tell the pharmacist.
- ☐ If the advice is for a child, tell the pharmacist the child's age.
- ☐ If the pharmacist suggests you should buy a medicine, ask how to take it and for how long.
- ☐ If you are not better after two or three days, you should go to your doctor.

If you have any questions about medicines, minor illnesses or other family health problems ask your pharmacist. You'll be taking good advice.

Produced by the National Pharmaceutical Association, the Pharmaceutical Services Negotiating Committee and the Pharmaceutical Society of Great Britain. 1 Lambeth High Street, London SE1 7JN. Tel: 01-735 9141.
Printed by Plain English Campaign, tel: 06633 4566.

---

### PHARMACY

### What to remember in a Pharmacy

Remember you can *always* talk to your pharmacist. Pharmacists are experts on medicines:

- ☐ they know how medicines are made, how they work and how they should be used
- ☐ they will tell you what is best for your cold or cough, your stomach ache or headache or any other minor illness
- ☐ they will also advise you about other health problems.

necessary? For instance, does 'When to take the medicine' need a clock next to it?

## The pamphlet's purpose

Is the pamphlet an advert? The pamphlet's purpose seems to be to show people how to take medicines safely.
Decide if it is also aimed at encouraging people to use a chemist sometimes instead of going to the doctor. What are you told about pharmacists (chemists) that is not true in every case? What image of the pharmacist is presented? Why, for instance, is he drawn wearing glasses?

## Make your own pamphlet

▭> Design a pamphlet of your own, using this one as a model. You might like to try one of these topics

How to get on at your school (a pamphlet for children when they first arrive).
How to keep pets (or just one pet).

Are you going to advertise your school in some way, stressing the best points, or are you going to write about the school's good and bad points?
Are you going to promote the keeping of pets in your pamphlet, or will your pamphlet be totally factual?

REMEMBER: People always write for a purpose, but writing has more than one purpose.

## ASSESSMENT

Prepare a Record Sheet on your pamphlet like the one on page 16. When assessing your pamphlet, be sure to include reactions to your design: any illustrations, use of colour, headings, different sized type.

— — — — — — — — — — — — — — — —

# Mr Willow teaches the exclamation mark!

(Mr Willow is an old-fashioned and strict teacher.)

'How old are you, Andrew?'

'Thirteen, Sir.'

'Well, when are you going to stop behaving like a three-year-old! Don't answer that, boy. It's not a question. It's an exclamation – of strong feeling – the feeling I get when I see you sneaking crisps out of your pocket all the time. You're like a grazing cow, boy! That's another exclamation. Now listen to this. Open the door. My hands are full. Sit down, Julie. I only meant it as an example. No exclamation marks needed. Not a strong feeling. Open the door! The room's on fire! Ho! That woke up Steven. No luck, boy. It was just an example. Strong feeling, so exclamation marks needed. Joel, will you shut your mouth! Why is it that whenever I open my mouth some idiot starts talking!

'Do you really want us to answer that, Sir?

'No, boy. It's an exclamation, not a question. Oh, I see what you mean. I put that rather badly.'

'What are you reading, Adeole? That's a question, by the way. Bring it here, at once! Exclamation, see. I'm cross with her. Ho! What have we here! A comic.'

'It's a magazine, Sir.'

'It's a silly comic – and here's a piece of luck. Full of exclamations. "Next day at the beauty contest. Oh, no! Just my luck! Lord Travers is one of the judges! That's curtains for me and Rupert! He'll never let his son marry someone in a beauty contest!"'

'Those are the thoughts of Beverley – see her here – soppy-looking girl – oh, and here are Lord Travers' thoughts in a big bubble.'

'"What a stunner!! Haven't I seen her somewhere before? Oh, no!! It's Rupert's fiancee! How could she lower herself!! I'll cut him off without a penny, if he marries her!!"'

'Millions of exclamations. And some double ones. Never use double exclamation marks. And don't use them all the time. Now listen! And look at me when I'm talking! Don't exclaim all the time! Got that! If you overuse exclamations they'll lose their force. Won't they, Benazir! Stop shuffling! Put your hand up, if you want something! Don't call out! Speak up, Joel! Don't look so worried! Now what do you want?'

'Does Rupert marry her in the end, Sir?'

'What! How dare you! That's it! That's the last straw! You'll never find out! Ugh! Ah! Into my cupboard it goes till the end of term. Now, get out, all of you!'

THEY WATCHED THE SUN SETTING. THE WHOLE SKY SEEMED ON FIRE.

⊂⊃ Mr Willow is fierce, sarcastic and very noisy. But he does know how *exclamation marks* should be used. In pairs, make up a set of rules, with examples, for the use of the exclamation mark. Compare your rules with others' and make any necessary alterations.

Do these as a check that you have understood:

1  Write a sentence of your own using one exclamation mark.
2  Write a short paragraph in which somebody shouts.
3  Draw a comic character and put in a *speech bubble* with more than one exclamation mark.
4  Write a sentence in which a teacher emphasises something.
5  Give an example of when Mr Willow is being sarcastic.

# Now listen carefully!

In what circumstances would you hear or read each of these?

Turn sharp right into Gresham Street and take the second left . . .

Beat two egg whites until stiff.

Open your books at page 23.

Move three squares, if you throw a six.

Take ONE after meals.

Ride about 60 cm from the edge of the road.

Break seal with a sharp knife.

Keep your bat straight when you play forward.

Life is full of *instructions*. To be good ones they must be clear and as short as possible. Look at the two pages from *A Highway Code for Young Road Users* on pages 24–25.

What can you learn about setting out instructions from these pages? Consider the language (Is it clear?), the use of numbered paragraphs, the use of capitals, the illustrations and the use of colour.

⊂⊃ In pairs, design instructions for *one* of these:

Pedestrian Crossings
Cycling in the Dark

Use all the features of the piece on cycling. Comment on the design and clarity of other pairs' work. Have you missed anything out?

## RIDING ALONG

**25.** You should not ride on the pavement unless there are special signs allowing you to do so.

**26.** Wheel your cycle to the edge of the kerb and if safe place it in the road. Get on your cycle and look all round for traffic even if you have a mirror fitted. When it is safe to move off signal with your right arm if necessary, and then with both hands on the handlebars cycle away.

**27.** Ride about 60cm from the edge of the road so that you avoid drains and gutters.

**28.** Always keep both hands on the handlebars unless you are signalling.

**29.** If riding with others on busy or narrow roads you should ride one behind the other. Never ride more than two side by side on any road.

**30.** Even if you are wheeling your cycle in the road, you must still obey traffic light signals and road signs. You must also obey the signals made by Police officers or Traffic wardens.

11

# Cycling

## RIDING ALONG

**31.** Never hold on to any vehicle or another cyclist.

**32.** You must not carry a passenger on your cycle.

**33.** You should never lead an animal whilst cycling.

**34.** Before turning right or left, overtaking, or stopping you must look behind and make sure it is safe. Give a clear arm signal to show what you intend to do. The signals that cyclists should give are:-

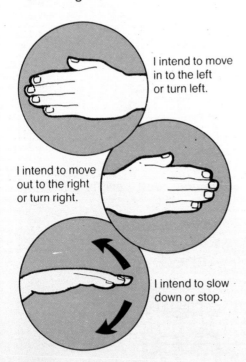

I intend to move in to the left or turn left.

I intend to move out to the right or turn right.

I intend to slow down or stop.

**35.** When turning from one road into another look out for pedestrians who may be crossing that road. Give way to them.

**36.** If you want to turn right from a busy road, moving to the middle of the road may be difficult and dangerous. It is often safer to stop on the left hand side and wait for a safe gap in the traffic before walking with your cycle across the road. This is especially important in the dark.

12

# Verbal instructions

How well can you remember and pass on a message? Imagine you have gone on holiday and forgotten to leave instructions for your neighbour's son, who has agreed to feed your cat. You telephone his home and leave this message with his mother:

'Please tell Ali that there are four tins of cat food in the cupboard to the right of the sink. The tin-opener is in the drawer next to the cooker. Give Tiddles half a tin in the morning and half at night. Leave him in at night but keep the doors shut so he doesn't get into the lounge and scratch the chairs.'

There are four *key points* for Ali's mother to remember.

Where the cat food is
Where the tin-opener is
How much to give Tiddles
A warning to shut doors

⇨ Work in groups of three. One of you prepare a message to be passed along. It could be similar to the message above or involve giving directions (where to meet, for instance) or passing on details of homework to be done. Make sure there are four key points to remember.
When everybody has prepared a message, work in your threes, one telephoning a message (mime using the telephone and don't look directly at each other) to be passed on to a third person who should preferably be out of earshot when the message is telephoned.
Try this in front of the class, the third person outside the room while the message is being given.
Check that the written message has been given in full. If not, where did it go wrong? Was it clear? Did the receiver listen carefully enough? Discuss this in a small group.

A war joke tells of a message that began at one end of a trench of soldiers as: 'Send reinforcements we're going to advance.' And it reached the other end as: 'Send three and fourpence we're going to a dance.'

## SPELL WELL

silly   illustrious   illusion   willing

afternoon   daft   crafty   drafting   re-draft

happened   frightened   opened   wizened

# USING THE DICTIONARY

## 3

Any writing that you do will be easier if you know your way around a dictionary. As we have said before, if you like words you will be good at English.
This Step is a guide to the dictionary.

Most writers write with a dictionary at their side. Few people can spell all the words found in one. Probably no one knows all the meanings of the words unless they are professional dictionary compilers. There are about 40,000 entries in the average school dictionary. The big Oxford dictionary printed in several books contains 500,000 entries.

## Make the dictionary your friend

Students sometimes don't use dictionaries because of:

1 the effort and the time it takes to look up a word
2 lack of success because a word is not always spelt as it sounds
3 the sheer number of words in a dictionary
4 not always understanding the meanings given
5 the hope they have guessed the spelling of a word correctly.

Your strategy is to get used to handling a dictionary until it becomes your friend. The hardest part is (2) finding words that are not spelt as they sound – for help with this you need to work closely with your teacher. Some dictionaries have a section on how words sound.

▭▷ Work in small groups. One of the group picks ten words from a dictionary.

The rest of the group race to find the words, writing down the page the words are on. The winner can choose the next ten words and so on. You will all need to use the same type of dictionary.

## Alphabetical order

Did you realise all the words in a dictionary are in **alphabetical order**? Do you really know what this means? Did you use the guide letters at the top of each page to help your search?

▷ Without using a dictionary put these words in alphabetical order:

carrier, anchor, bus, ghost, egg, farmer.
Explain how you did it.

dregs, dingy, damp, duty, dear, dwindle, dope.
Explain how you did it.

rock, rod, routine, road, roller, robbery, roguery.
Explain how you did it.

scatter, scavenge, scale, scaffold, scabies, scapula, scald.
Explain how you did it.

## What words mean

Trying to **define** a word (say what it means) is not easy.

▷ In small groups define these words and then check them with their meanings given in a dictionary.

| | |
|---|---|
| bicycle | head |
| egg | nail |
| silly | basket |
| rude | candle |
| microscope | messy |

What did you do if there was more than

one meaning? How many do you think each meaning would score, if it was out of 3?

▷ On your own, look for words of more than one meaning. Normally they are listed 1, 2, 3, 4, etc. in a dictionary. Who can find the most meanings for one word? Spend twenty minutes on this.

## Parts of speech

A dictionary will tell you which **part of speech** a word is:

| | | |
|---|---|---|
| *n* | = | noun |
| *v* | = | verb |
| *adj* | = | adjective |
| *adv* | = | adverb |
| *conj* | = | conjunction |
| *prep* | = | preposition |
| *pron* | = | pronoun |

▷ Which words on this page of a dictionary can be more than one part of speech? Make a list.

# poi

**poignant** *adj* **1** producing a sharp feeling of sadness **2** (of sorrow) deeply felt △ PUNGENT — ~**ly** *adv* — **-nancy** *n*

**point¹** *n* **1** a sharp end **2** a piece of land with a sharp end that stretches into the sea **3 a** also **decimal point**— a sign (·) separating a whole number from decimals: *When we read out 4·23 we say '4 point 2 3 '* **b** a full stop **4** (in geometry) an imaginary place that has position but no size **5 a** place: *The bus stops at 4 or 5 points along this road* **6** an exact moment: *It was at that point that I left* **7** also **point of the compass**— **a** any of the 32 marks on a compass, showing direction **b** any of the equal divisions (each of 11° 15′) between any 2 of these **8** a degree of temperature: *the melting point of gold* **9** a measure of increase or decrease in cost, value, etc. **10** a single quantity used in deciding the winner in games: *We won by 12 points to 3* **11** the meaning of something said or done: *I didn't see the point of his remark* **12** a noticeable quality or ability: *Work isn't her strong point* **13** purpose; use: *There's no point in wasting time* **14** also **power point**— a fixed socket into which a plug can be fitted to connect an apparatus to the supply of electricity **15** (in cricket) (the fielder in) a position directly facing the batsman and about half way to the edge of the playing area

**point²** *v* **1** to hold out a finger, a stick, etc., in a direction **2** to aim, direct, or turn **3** to fill the spaces between the bricks of (a wall) with mortar or cement **4** (of a dog) to show where (a hunted animal or bird) is —see POINTER **5** to bring (the toes) to a point by bending the ankles forward

**point-blank** *adj, adv* **1** from a close position level with the object: *a point-blank shot* **2** forceful and direct: *a point-blank refusal*

**point duty** *n* the controlling of traffic by a policeman usu. at a point where 2 roads cross

**pointed** *adj* **1** shaped to a point: *pointed fingernails* **2** directed in a noticeable unfriendly way: *a pointed remark* **3** sharply expressed or shown (esp. in the phrase **pointed wit**) — ~**ly** *adv*

**pointer** *n* **1** a stick used to point at things on a map, board, etc. **2** the needle that points to the numbers on a measuring apparatus **3** a hunting dog that stops with its nose pointed towards a hunted animal or bird it has smelt **4** a useful suggestion

**pointless** *adj* **1** meaningless **2** useless; unnecessary — ~**ly** *adv* — ~**ness** *n*

**point of order** *n* **points of order** a matter connected with the organization of an official meeting

**point of view** also **viewpoint**— *n* **points of view** a way of considering or judging a thing, person, etc.: *From my point of view it would be better to come tomorrow*

**point out** *v adv* to draw attention to

**points** *n* **1 2** short rails moved to allow a train to change tracks **2** the ends of the toes, as danced on in ballet **3** a horse's feet, tail, and mane, or a cat's legs, tail, and face, where these differ from the body colour **4** the bodily qualities considered in judging an animal in a show

**pointsman** *n* **-men** a railway worker in charge of the moving of points

**point to** also **point towards**— *v prep* to be a sign of

**point-to-point** *n* **-points** a cross-country horse-race, usu. with points marked along the way

**poise¹** *v* **poised**, **poising** to balance in an unsteady position

**poise²** *n* **1** good judgment and quiet confidence: *He has a great deal of poise for a boy of only 14* **2** the way of holding oneself: *the dancer's graceful poise*

**poised** *adj* **1** in a condition of uncertainty: *poised between life and death* **2** having poise **3** still, as if hanging, in the air: *The bee hung poised above the flower* **4** lightly seated: *poised on the edge of a chair* **5** in a state of readiness to act or move: *poised for action*

**poison¹** *n* **1** a substance that harms or kills if an animal or plant takes it in **2** an evil or unwanted influence

**poison²** *v* **1** to give poison to; harm or kill with poison **2** to put poison into or onto (something) **3** to infect: *a poisoned foot* **4** to make dangerously impure: *Chemicals are poisoning our rivers* **5** to influence in a harmful or evil way: *She poisoned her husband's mind against his sister* — ~**er** *n*

**poisonous** *adj* **1** containing poison: *poisonous snakes* **2** having the effects of poison: *This substance is poisonous* **3** harmful to the mind; evil: *poisonous ideas* **4** very unpleasant: *a poisonous green colour* — ~**ly** *adv*

**poison-pen letter** *n* a usu. unsigned letter making charges of misbehaviour, or saying bad things about someone

**poke¹** *n* **(buy) a pig in a poke** *esp. spoken* (to buy) something which one has not seen, and which may prove worthless

**poke²** *v* **poked**, **poking** **1** to push sharply out of or through an opening: *His elbow was poking through his sleeve* **2** to push (a pointed thing) into (someone or something) **3** to move the wood into (a fire) with a poker or other such or coal about in (a fire) by pushing, forcing, object **4** to make (a hole) by pushing, forcing, etc. **5** *esp. spoken* to hit with the hand closed **6 poke fun at** to make jokes against **7 poke one's nose into something** *esp. spoken* to enquire into something that does not concern one

**poke³** *n* **1** an act of poking with something pointed **2** *esp. spoken* a blow with the closed hand: *He took a poke at his opponent*

**poker¹** *n* a thin metal bar used to poke a fire to make it burn better

**poker²** *n* a card game usu. played for money

**poker face** *n* a face that shows nothing of a person's thoughts or feelings — **poker-faced** *adj*

**pokerwork** *n* ornamentation or the art of ornamenting wood or leather by burning the surface with hot instruments

# FOOTNOTE

# SPELL WELL

The front part of a dictionary explains how to use it. Read through it.
The back part of a dictionary normally contains useful lists like weights and measures. It should also contain a list of **prefixes** (word beginnings) and **suffixes** (word endings). In the Longman *New Generation Dictionary* these are listed as beginnings and endings on pages 784–786.

▭ On your own, make a word that begins:

aero, anti, bio, equi, micro, photo.

Make a word that ends:

able, gram, graph, ish, logy, ous, ship.

A dictionary is useful to find the meaning of expressions.

▭ What do these mean?

to split hairs (look under s)
the apple of someone's eye (a)
sit on the fence (f)
come under the hammer (h)
(put something) on the map (m)

interest   pint   winter   interact   splinter

asteroid   casting   disaster   plaster

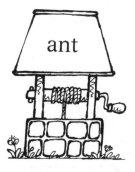

currant (which one)?   distant   attendant   radiant

(This is a tricky one. Check in your dictionary to see if the ending is 'ant' or 'ent'.)

# VERB POWER AND SENTENCES

You can drive a car without knowing anything about a car engine. But you are a better driver if you do. What if you break down, for instance?

You can write a sentence without knowing anything about the parts of speech. But you can sometimes write a better sentence if you do. A sentence can break down like a car, and then it is handy to know what its parts are. The most important part – and the hardest – is the verb. In this Step we look at verbs.

## Working with words

⇨ Look at this recipe and then write a recipe of your own. It doesn't matter if it doesn't work. You can use the opportunity to make a silly recipe – a match-stick pie, for instance – but you must set it out clearly.

### Chilled Cucumber And Coriander Soup
*A light and refreshing summertime soup.*

1 large cucumber, washed, peeled and grated.

1 tablespoonful (15 ml) white wine vinegar.

1 tablespoonful sugar.

2 tablespoonfuls coriander, chopped.

Juice of ½ lemon.

½ small onion, peeled and finely chopped.

6 tablespoonfuls (90 ml) Heinz Mayonnaise.

½ pint (300 ml) cold water.

Salt and freshly-ground black pepper.

Strips of cucumber peel and coriander leaves, to garnish.

Serves 4.

Place the cucumber, vinegar and sugar in a bowl, and leave to marinade for 2 hours. Blend in the coriander, lemon juice, onion, mayonnaise, water and seasoning. Chill well and transport to your picnic site in a chilled vacuum flask. Decorate with cucumber peel and coriander leaves.

Look at the sentences below the list of ingredients for Cucumber Soup. They begin with the instruction words – *Place, Blend, Chill, Decorate.*
Your recipe probably began in the same way with the same kinds of words, for example, *Take, Mix, Peel* . . .
They are the action words – **verbs**.

Nouns, pronouns and adjectives are the parts of speech we studied in *New Steps, Book 1.*
But the most important part of speech is the verb. You cannot make a sentence without a verb.

## *Re-cap: parts of speech you already know*

Read the following silly sentences.

1 From a report about a gun being found in a passenger's bag on an aeroplane:
'He claims he has never seen it before and that she must have placed it in it before he carried it onto it. When it took off and they searched it he was amazed that they found it there.'

2 From an estate agent's advert:
'It is a house with windows and a garden on a road in a part of the town.'

3 From a report on an incident at school:
'Rebecca told Mark that if Mark did not stop following Rebecca home and shouting at Rebecca, Rebecca would fetch Rebecca's dad to deal with Mark.'

▭▷ Decide which of these comments fits which sentence and then re-write the sentences.

1 Haven't you ever heard of **pronouns**? You've used one noun five times in a sentence.
2 I can't tell who's who and what's what! Let's have some names, a few **nouns**.
3 Will this really attract customers? I don't think so. **Adjectives** are our stock-in-trade. Let's have 'large', 'attractive', 'quiet', 'secluded', 'spacious'.

# Learning to use sentences

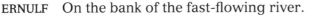In pairs, read this short play called 'So What Happened?'.

## So What Happened?

SCENE: A cave in very ancient Britain. Cavewoman Ivo is sitting in the entrance peeling rabbits. Enter Caveman Ernulf.

| | |
|---|---|
| IVO | Morning, Ernulf. You look as if you have been running. |
| ERNULF | On the bank of the fast-flowing river. |
| IVO | Go on! |
| ERNULF | Underneath the hanging grey rock. |
| IVO | Are you all right? |
| ERNULF | The wolf near Egbert's house. |
| IVO | What about it? |

| ERNULF | The wolf with the floppy ears and the curled-up tail. |
|---|---|
| IVO | Yes, I know it. It howls in a high-pitched tuneful sort of way. |
| ERNULF | Your son Wulfram with the red hair and spots. |
| IVO | Freckles they are, but never mind. What about him? |
| ERNULF | The tree on the rock near the fast-flowing river. |
| IVO | I think you ought to see the cave doctor. You aren't making any sense. Tell me something – about the tree, the river, the rock, my son or the wolf. Anything, but for your own sake – you won't be the first man I've peeled – make a statement. |
| ERNULF | Your red-haired, freckled son climbed the tree on the rock near the fast-flowing river. |
| IVO | Well done. Say on. More! More! |
| ERNULF | He fell out of the tree. |
| IVO | I'll kill him for climbing trees. |
| ERNULF | There is no need to do that. The wolf with the floppy ears and the curled-up tail has eaten him. |

Until Ivo threatens Ernulf with her rabbit-peeling knife he says groups of words that don't make any sense. He doesn't speak in *sentences*.

A sentence is a group of words that makes sense in itself.

▭ Here are ten groups of words. Which ones would annoy Ivo? Add words to those which need them to make them into sentences.

1  Green grass.
2  Trees drop their leaves in autumn.
3  While I prepared the meal, my mother laid the table.
4  Are you going out?
5  Six ice-creams.
6  It grows quickly.
7  The rusty old bicycle.
8  The car was found in a barn.
9  In the park.
10  Listen to me!

## Make startling sentences

When Ernulf finally starts making sentences he ends up with a very dramatic one.

▭ Add to each group of words below to make a surprising or funny sentence. The first one is done for you.

1  Your new car . . .
   Your new car has rolled over the cliff top and is floating towards France.
2  The record-player you lent me . . .
3  The school caretaker . . .
4  When I put my foot in the water . . .
5  A big brussel-sprout . . .
6  My Uncle Imran . . .
7  I looked up and saw . . .
8  The referee blew the whistle as . . .
9  He was only fourteen but . . .
10  The star was rushing . . .

Compare your sentences with others in the class. Who has made the most surprising or the funniest one?

## Ernulf's long sentence

To make up for not speaking to Ivo in sentences, Ernulf went home and told his wife the news in the longest sentence in Cave history. Here it is:

'By the fast-flowing river, underneath the hanging rock with the tree on top, a grey wolf with the curled-up tail from near Egbert's ate the red-haired, freckled boy called Wulfram, the second son of Ivo and Cuthbert.'
'You could have told me that in four words,' said Ernulf's wife.
'Criticism, that's all I get,' said Ernulf. 'What four words?'

What were the four words?

▭ Cut these sentences to the number of words in brackets after each one. Make sure each still makes a sensible statement and is still a sentence.

1 The next morning Nazma looked through the rain-spattered window and saw the man the police had been looking for. (5)

2 Underneath the old photograph album in the top drawer of the desk the man eventually found the will his father had made many years ago. (5)

In making your three short sentences you will have had to keep some noun words such as 'wolf' and 'Egbert', but two words you couldn't manage without are *saw* and *found*. These are the action words – the verbs.

REMEMBER: Without a verb you cannot make a sentence.

▭ Make these groups of words into sentences. You will find in each case that you have used a verb.

    A five-pound note
    The one in the middle with the pink
        wrapping
    The dog in the corner
    After a large meal
    Under the settee

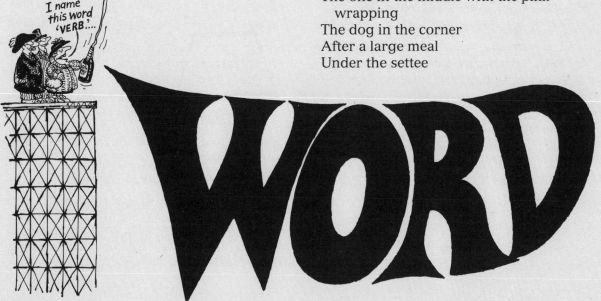

I name this word 'VERB'...

WORD

## Spot the sentence

We speak and write in sentences, groups of words that make a definite statement.
In writing we have ways of showing where the sentences begin and end. What are they?

*SPELL WELL*

fortunately   freely   widely   lonely

courage   outrage   page   carriage

beautiful   careful   hopeful   awful

(English words end in 'ful', not 'full')

# STORIES FROM THE PAST

## 5

In your National Curriculum course you
will read many modern stories. But you will
also be expected to look at some stories
from the past.
Here we ask you to look at a myth and then
to continue it as a story of your own.

## Myths and legends

The earliest stories are *myths* and *legends*,
like the stories about King Arthur. We
believe that they were first told orally and
later written down.
As well as being good stories – they must
be as they have lasted so many years – they
often attempt to explain the world and its
history. Imagine being a young Greek girl
or boy and hearing this story 2000 years
ago for the first time.
One of the problems of reading old stories
is that the names of the characters and
places can be difficult to say. So here is a
guide to the pronunciation in this myth:

| | |
|---|---|
| Priam | pry-am |
| Athamas | ath-am-ass |
| Asclepius | as-cleep-e-us |
| Aphrodite | a-fro-die-tee |
| Nephele | nef-ee-lee |
| Phrixus | frix-us |
| Helle | hell-ay |
| Hermes | her-mees |
| Perseus | per-say-us |
| Phoenician | fun-ee-shun |
| Ino | ee-no |
| Pytho | pie-though |
| Hellespont | hell-es-pont |
| Euxine | yux-seen-ay |
| Colchis | col-chis |
| Aeëtes | a-eat-tees |
| Circe | sir-say |

# The Children of the Cloud

While Troy still stood fast, and before King Priam was born, there was a king called Athamas, who reigned in a country beside the Grecian sea. Athamas was a young man, and was unmarried because none of the princesses who then lived seemed to him beautiful enough to be his wife. One day he left his palace and climbed high up into a mountain, following the course of a little river. He came to a place where a great black rock stood on one side of the river, jutting into the stream. Round the rock the water flowed deep and dark. Yet, through the noise of the river, the king thought he heard laughter and voices like the voices of girls. So he climbed very quietly up the back of the rock, and, looking over the edge, there he saw three beautiful maidens bathing in a pool, and splashing each other with the water. Their long yellow hair covered them like cloaks and floated behind them on the pool. One of them was even more beautiful than the others, and as soon as he saw her the king fell in love with her, and said to himself, 'This is the wife for me.'

As he thought this, his arm touched a stone, which slipped from the top of the rock where he lay, and went leaping, faster and faster as it fell, till it dropped with a splash into the pool below. Then the three maidens heard it, and were frightened, thinking someone was near. So they rushed out of the pool to the grassy bank where their clothes lay, lovely soft clothes, white and grey, and rosy-coloured, all shining with pearl drops, and diamonds like dew.

In a moment they had dressed, and then it was as if they had wings, for they rose gently from the ground, and floated softly up and up the windings of the brook. Here and there among the green tops of the mountain-ash trees the king could just see the white robes shining and disappearing, and shining again, till they rose far off like a mist, and so up and up into the sky, and at last he only followed them with his eyes, as they floated like clouds among the other clouds across the blue. All day he watched them, and at sunset he saw them sink, golden and rose-coloured and purple, and go down into the dark with the setting sun.

The king went home to his palace, but he was very unhappy, and nothing gave him any pleasure. All day he roamed about among the hills, and looked for the beautiful girls, but he never found them, and all night he dreamed about them, till he grew thin and pale and was like to die.

Now, the way with sick men then was that they made a pilgrimage to the temple of a god, and in the temple they offered sacrifices. Then they hoped that the god would appear to them in a dream, or send them a true dream at least, and tell them how they might be made well again. So the king drove in his chariot a long way, to the town where this temple was. When he reached it, he found it a strange place. The priests were dressed in dogs' skins, with the heads of the dogs drawn down over their faces, and there were live dogs running all about the shrines, for they were the favourite beasts of the god, whose name was Asclepius. There was an image of him, with a dog crouched at his feet, and in his hand he held a serpent, and fed it from a bowl.

The king sacrificed before the god, and when night fell he was taken into the temple, and there were many beds strewn on the floor and many people lying on them, both rich and poor, hoping that the god would appear to them in a dream, and tell them how they might be healed. There the king lay, like the rest, and for long he could not close his eyes. At length he slept, and he dreamed a dream. But it was not the god of the temple that he saw in his dream; he saw a beautiful lady, she seemed to float above him in a chariot drawn by doves, and all about her was a crowd of chattering sparrows, and he knew that she was Aphrodite, the Queen of Love. She was more beautiful than any woman in the world, and she smiled as she looked at the king, and said, 'Oh, King Athamas, you are sick for love! Now this you must do: go home and on the first night of the new moon, climb the hills to that place where you saw the Three Maidens. In the dawn they will come again to the river, and bathe in the pool. Then do you creep out of the wood, and steal the clothes of her you love, and she will not be able to fly away with the rest, and she will be your wife.'

Then she smiled again, and her doves bore her away, and the king woke, and remembered the dream, and thanked the lady in his heart, for he knew that she was a goddess, the Queen of Love.

Then he drove home, and did all that he had been told to do. On the first night of the new moon, when she shines like a thin gold thread in the sky, he left his palace, and climbed up through the hills, and hid in the wood by the edge of the pool. When the dawn began to shine silvery, he heard voices, and saw the three girls come floating through the trees, and alight on the river bank, and undress, and run into the water. There they bathed, and splashed each other with the water, laughing in their play. Then he stole to the grassy bank, and seized the clothes of the most beautiful of the three; and they heard him move, and rushed out to their clothes. Two of them were clad in a moment, and floated away up the glen, but the third crouched sobbing and weeping under the thick cloak of her yellow hair. Then she prayed the king to give her back her soft grey and rose-coloured raiment, but he would not till she had promised to be his wife. And he told her how long he had loved her, and how the goddess had sent him to be her husband, and at last she promised, and took his hand, and in her shining robes went down the hill with him to the palace. But he felt as if he walked on the air, and she scarcely seemed to touch the ground with her feet. She told him that her name was Nephele, which meant 'a cloud', in their language, and that she was one of the Cloud Fairies, who bring the rain, and live on the hilltops, and in the high lakes, and water springs, and in the sky.

So they were married, and lived very happily, and had two children, a boy called Phrixus, and a daughter named Helle. The two children had a beautiful pet, a Ram with a fleece all of gold, which was given them by the young god

called Hermes, a beautiful god, with wings on his shoon*, – for these were the very Shoon of Swiftness, that he lent afterwards to the boy, Perseus, who slew the Gorgon, and took her head. This Ram the children used to play with, and they would ride on his back, and roll about with him on the flowery meadows.

They would all have been happy, but for one thing. When there were clouds in the sky, and when there was rain, then their mother, Nephele, was always with them; but when the summer days were hot and cloudless, then she went away, they did not know where. The long dry days made her grow pale and thin, and, at last, she would vanish altogether, and never come again, till the sky grew soft and grey with rain.

King Athamas grew weary of this, for often his wife would be long away. Besides there was a very beautiful girl called Ino, a dark girl, who had come in a ship of Phoenician merchantmen, and had stayed in the city of the king when her friends sailed from Greece. The king saw her, and often she would be at the palace, playing with the children when their mother had disappeared with the Clouds, her sisters.

This Ino was a witch, and one day she put a drug into the king's wine, and when he had drunk it, he quite forgot Nephele, his wife, and fell in love with Ino. At last he married her, and they had two children, a boy and a girl, and Ino wore the crown, and was queen, and gave orders that Nephele should never be allowed to enter the palace any more. So Phrixus and Helle never saw their mother, and they were dressed in ragged old skins of deer, and were ill fed, and were set to do hard work in the house, while the children of Ino wore gold crowns in their hair, and were dressed in fine raiment, and had the best of everything.

One day when Phrixus and Helle were in the field, herding the sheep (for now they were treated like peasant children, and had to work for their bread), they met an old woman, all wrinkled, and poorly clothed, and they took pity on her, and brought her home with them. Queen Ino saw her, and as she wanted a nurse for her own children, she took her in to be the nurse, and the old woman had charge of the children, and lived in the house, and she was kind to Phrixus and Helle. But neither of them knew that she was their own mother, Nephele, who had disguised herself as an old woman and a servant, that she might be with her children.

Phrixus and Helle grew strong and tall, and more beautiful than Ino's children, so she hated them, and determined, at last, to kill them. They all slept at night in one room, but Ino's children had gold crowns in their hair, and beautiful coverlets on their beds. One night, Phrixus was half awake, and he heard the old nurse come, in the dark, and put something on his head, and on his sister's, and change their coverlets. But he was so drowsy that he half thought it was a dream, and he lay and fell asleep. In the dead of night, the wicked stepmother, Ino, crept into the room with a dagger in her hand, and she stole up to the bed of Phrixus, and felt his hair, and his coverlet. Then she

* *shoon* – shoes

went softly to the bed of Helle, and felt her coverlet, and her hair with the gold crown on it. So she supposed those to be her own children, and she kissed them in the dark, and went to the beds of the other two children. She felt their heads, and they had no crowns on, so she killed them, supposing that they were Phrixus and Helle. Then she crept downstairs and went back to bed.

In the morning, there lay the stepmother Ino's children cold and dead, and nobody knew who had killed them. Only the wicked queen knew, and she, of course, would not tell of herself, but if she hated Phrixus and Helle before, now she hated them a hundred times worse than ever. But the old nurse was gone; nobody ever saw her there again, and everybody but the queen thought that *she* had killed the two children. Everywhere the king sought for her, to burn her alive, but he never found her, for she had gone back to her sisters, the Clouds.

And the Clouds were gone, too! For six long months, from winter to harvest time, the rain never fell. The country was burned up, the trees grew black and dry, there was no water in the streams, the corn turned yellow and died before it was come into the ear. The people were starving, the cattle and sheep were perishing, for there was no grass. And every day the sun rose hot and red, and went blazing through the sky without a cloud.

Here the wicked stepmother, Ino, saw her chance. The king sent messengers to Pytho, to consult the prophetess, and to find out what should be done to bring back the clouds and the rain. Then Ino took the messengers, before they set out on their journey, and gave them gold, and threatened also to kill them, if they did not bring the message she wished from the prophetess. Now this message was that Phrixus and Helle must be burned as a sacrifice to the gods.

So the messengers went, and came back dressed in mourning. And when they were brought before the king, at first they would tell him nothing. But he commanded them to speak, and then they told him, not the real message from the prophetess, but what Ino had bidden them to say: that Phrixus and Helle must be offered as a sacrifice to appease the gods.

The king was very sorrowful at this news, but he could not disobey the gods. So poor Phrixus and Helle were wreathed with flowers, as sheep used to be when they were led to be sacrificed, and they were taken to the altar, all the people following and weeping, and the Golden Ram went between them, as they walked to the temple. Then they came within sight of the sea, which lay beneath the cliff where the temple stood, all glittering in the sun, and the happy white sea-birds flying over it.

Here the Ram stopped, and suddenly he spoke to Phrixus, for the god gave him utterance, and said: 'Lay hold of my horn, and get on my back, and let Helle climb up behind you, and I will carry you far away.'

Then Phrixus took hold of the Ram's horn, and Helle mounted behind him, and grasped the golden fleece, and suddenly the Ram rose in the air, and flew above the people's heads, far away over the sea.

Far away to the eastward he flew, and deep below them they saw the sea,

and the islands, and the white towers and temples, and the fields, and ships. Eastward always he went, toward the sun-rising, and Helle grew dizzy and weary. At last a deep sleep came over her, and she let go her hold of the Fleece, and fell from the Ram's back, down and down, into the narrow seas that run between Europe and Asia, and there she was drowned. And that strait is called Helle's Ford, or Hellespont, to this day.

But Phrixus and the Ram flew on up the narrow seas, and over the great sea which the Greeks called the Euxine and we call the Black Sea, till they reached a country named Colchis. There the Ram alighted, so tired and weary that he died, and Phrixus had his beautiful Golden Fleece stripped off, and hung on an oak tree in a dark wood. And there it was guarded by a monstrous Dragon, so that nobody dared to go near it. And Phrixus married the king's daughter, and lived long, till he died also, and a king called Aeëtes, the brother of the enchantress, Circe, ruled that country. Of all the things he had, the rarest was the Golden Fleece, and it became a proverb that nobody could take that Fleece away, nor deceive the Dragon who guarded it.

▭ Discuss how you would know that this is a myth or a legend, if you had not been told.

1 What sort of people does it deal with?
2 What kind of adventures do they have?
3 What magical or supernatural things happen in it?
4 How are natural things like drought explained?

## Continue the myth

Look at the last sentence. Somebody is bound to try to take the fleece from King Aeëtes. You may even have heard of Jason. He is tricked by a wicked king to go in search of it. Greece is a land of many islands and Jason has many adventures as he goes in search of it. Remember too that it is guarded by a dragon that must be lured away if anyone is to get the fleece. King Aeëtes has a beautiful daughter with strange powers called Medea (Med-ee-à). She could help Jason.

▭ On your own, continue the myth of the golden fleece. You could think of it as a cartoon film that needed a voice-over script. If you do it this way, you need not draw the pictures. You need only to explain what is in each picture like this:

| *Picture* | *Voice Over* |
|---|---|
| Jason's boat in a storm | Jason and his crew had to row through the worst storms ever seen in Greece. The winds were the breath of a sea god. |

Check your story against the real one of 'Jason and the Golden Fleece' from your library.

quarter   inquire   require   acquire

display   inlay   allay   underlay

olden   gold   scold   boldest

# GHOSTLY HAPPENINGS

## 6

Some people think newspapers are myths –
they tell about things that never happened.
Do you believe what you read in
newspapers? Can we say: 'It's in the paper;
it must be true'? Do papers exaggerate?
If you are not a newspaper reader, it is time
you started to look at bits that interest you.
It will help your English.

## Be a reporter

⇨ Read the newspaper article on page
**46** (from the *Daily Mirror*, 19 January 1989).

1 Do you believe this story?
2 What 'hauntings' are there? List them.
3 When did the 'hauntings' happen?
4 Why have we put 'hauntings' in inverted
   commas?
5 Why might there be no complaints from
   the new tenants?
6 Would you like the story of the ghostly
   happenings to be true?

## Write a summary

⇨ You wish to re-write this article for the
school magazine or newspaper. But you
can only have 200 words. What will you put
in and what will you leave out?

## Write a ghost story

⇨ Using the article from **page 46** as a
basis, make up a story (fiction) called: 'The
Haunted Council House' or 'Nottingham
Ghost'. Imagine you are staying in the
house.

# THE HAUNTED HOUSE

- ● **Invisible fingers tapped out words on typewriter**
- ● **Ghostly music played on children's toy organ**
- ● **Lawyer was levitated out of his bed by spirits**

RIDDLE: The council semi where a family were driven out by "ghosts".

By GEORGINA WALSH

A "TERRIFIED" solicitor's clerk told yesterday of the night he was levitated from his bed in a haunted house.

He said he also heard ghostly music from a child's toy organ and saw a message being typed by "an invisible hand".

Down-to-earth Yorkshireman Jack Yates, 64, now retired from his legal post, said: "I felt this force lift me about a foot in the air.

*"It seemed to last for several minutes. I had to use all my strength to come down again."*

Mr Yates said he had been sceptical about a couple's claims that their Nottingham council house was haunted.

WITNESS: Jack Yates

But he was so unnerved by his experience he fled to the next room where John and Helen Costello were huddled together with their family.

And it persuaded him to give evidence for the couple who have taken Nottingham city council to the High Court in London in an attempt to be rehoused.

*If they win their case, it will make legal history.*

## Moved

The frightened Costellos and their daughters Rosie, 14, Susie, 19, and Sharon, 21, moved out of the "spooky semi" in Melbourne Road, Aspley, after just four months — unable to take any more.

But the council ruled they had intentionally made themselves homeless and refused to rehouse them.

The family are now living in bed and breakfast accommodation.

*They claim they were spooked by five spirits — including the "mischievous one".*

The court heard that the council never investigated their claims first hand, even though police and social workers were notified.

Mr Yates said he was a friend of the family and agreed to sleep in a downstairs living room to check their story.

Speaking after the court reserved judge-

HOMELESS: John and Helen Costello and daughters Rose (left) and Susie

ment in the case, he described how the light in his room started to switch itself off and on.

Then suddenly he was physically levitated and had to struggle desperately to get back down.

Next he saw the typewriter start to move. He said:

❝ It was as if invisible fingers were pressing the keys. Then the paper started scrambling itself.

I grabbed the paper and right across it were the letters AH, AH, AH.

I witnessed it ❞ with my own eyes.

Mr Yates said the ghostly music appeared to come from a child's toy organ which was not plugged in and had no batteries.

He also heard scratching on his bedclothes and strange knockings in the air.

## Blessed

Mr Yates said he taped the noises on a pocket recorder. But when he tried to play it back, there was just silence. He added:

❝ A Catholic priest came to bless the house. He sprinkled holy water and it sprayed back all over us.

It would be impossible

for someone to live there and remain ❞ sane.

The Costellos moved into the house after it had been specially adapted so that Sharon, who is handicapped, could live with them.

But they say that as soon as Sharon stepped over the threshold, a noise like "a gigantic heartbeat" sent her into such a state that she had to be taken to hospital.

Finally they fled the house, without even taking their possessions.

The council claims it has had no complaints from the new tenants.

## 'I couldn't stay sane there'

46

Read 'Spooked by a ghostly sobbing' (*Daily Mail,* 11 February 1989). Do you think there is always a natural explanation for something described as ghostly? Imagine the wife is on her own one night in a high wind. What does she tell the Press? Write it down as it might appear in a newspaper.

# Spooked by a ghostly sobbing

WE have a pretty noisy house: It creaks and groans, it sighs and knocks.

Twice this week we have had huge winds and, at the height of the howling storm, the house suddenly produced an entirely new sound, in the downstairs cloakroom of all places. It was a two-banded kind of noise, like a great sobbing chord played on two strings of a giant cello in some hellish orchestra.

Inside and outside the room, it moaned. What on earth was it? I waited until the morning to seek its source.

At first I was utterly foxed. And then I saw it. Or rather, them. Two drainpipes were the source of the noise.

They must have operated like two giant organ pipes, the air blowing in at the bottom and out at the top, making the pipes sing and scream in unison. My wife is unconvinced; but then she believes in ghosts.

## FOOTNOTE

To be a reporter you have to take notes, **especially of what people say.** (See page 110 if you want to know more about taking notes.) You then have to decide whether you are going to write down what was said to you as either *direct* or *reported speech.* Look at the beginning of the article on page 46:

'I felt this force lift me about a foot in the air.'

This is *direct speech.* It is word-for-word what Mr Yates said. Notice that speech marks (*inverted commas*) are used.

Mr Yates said he had been sceptical about a couple's claims that their Nottingham council house was haunted.

This is *reported speech.* Notice that you do not need speech marks as you are not putting down the actual words used. Notice also that you report in the past using the *past tense* (the past time).

## Role play 1

▭ Divide into groups of four or five. Each group is a family to whom something sad, happy or exciting has recently happened. Decide what the event is. Make sure that everyone in the group knows the details. Then meet another group. Take it in turns to be reporters and the family. Interview the family groups in turn, then write up each others' stories as newspaper articles. Before you begin, look at the dramatic headings in the council house ghost article. You will need some dramatic headings in your article too. Also, look again at the use of direct speech and reported speech in the article. As reporters, try to get interesting quotations (quotes) from the family members.

## Role play 2

Keep the same family groups, but re-organise if necessary to make an even number so that the groups can work together.

There has been a quarrel between two families. Family A has a large dog that Family B thinks has dug up some recently planted bulbs in their garden. Family A claims the dog has never been into Family B's garden. There has already been much argument and unpleasantness. Now there has been a fight between two of the children.

Begin your role play with the children going back to their families, telling their versions of the fight.

Each family decides what is to be done. At some time they, or representatives from each family, will meet.

▭ On your own, write a fair report of the meeting for your local press. After you have done it discuss as a group how difficult it was to be fair and not to take sides.

## SPELL WELL

sieve   believe   retrieve   grieve

receive   height   weight   conceive

disappear   disaster   disappoint   discover

# THE POWER
# OF THE VERB

7

There is more to learn about verbs than we told you in Step 4. Here we have another look at them.

We may surprise you in this Step by showing you that you know more verbs than you think and, therefore, you can write better than you thought.

Mr Willow returns to teach some uses of the comma.

## The making of a sentence

Look at these lists of words:

A boat man desk girl idea sea house monster
B large good young red old happy
C ran escaped lived thought knew sailed worked saw
D carefully quickly near hard away easily
E in on by from to under beneath
F and but if when who though
G you he she they us me

A prize for anybody who can make a sentence from *one* of these groups of words.

No, it can't be done.

Each group contains words of the *same sort*. Each group is one part of speech.

So far we have learned about nouns, pronouns, adjectives and verbs. Under which letters do these four parts of speech come in the lists above?

Sentences are made by using different parts of speech. You fit different kinds of words together to make a sentence. Here's one using a word from each of the groups above (You are allowed to add *the, a* or *an*):

A young girl lived near the sea and she sailed an old red boat.

▭ Try to make three sentences for yourself by using one or more words from each group. Here is a start:

The old man ran away when . . .

*49*

# Verbs control what happens

Group C are the action words – verbs. You can't make a sentence without one of them. They control what happens in the sentence – and when it happens.

Did you notice that all the sentences you made up happened in the past; this was because all the verbs were in the past tense form.

Now don't get tense about tense. Tense just means time. There are three main times: past, present and future. To bring the 'young girl' of our sentence alive we need to change the verbs to the *present tense*:

A young girl *lives* near the sea and *sails* an old red boat.

▭ Change your three sentences so that the events are happening now. Put all the verbs into the present tense.

To put our sentence into the future we need to do this:

A young girl *will live* near the sea and she *will sail* an old red boat.

▭ Put your sentences into the *future tense*.

You use the three tenses quite naturally during speech. All we have done is to show you which is which in writing.

▭ Discuss verb tenses. What did you notice about the way verbs form tenses? Look at the end of them, or in the case of the future, the word or words that come before them. Make a list of any questions you would like to ask your teacher about tense.

## Change the tense

▭ Look back at the newspaper article on the haunted house. Imagine you have gone to see the house for yourself to interview the new occupants for a local radio station. While you are there something unusual happens. Describe it in your report. There are two parts to your report. The first is in the house, and might begin:

'Mrs James is showing me round the house. The typewriter is still here. It looks ordinary enough . . .'

After the unusual event – you can make it hair-raising, if you like (Mrs James has levitated and is stuck on the ceiling), you complete your report outside, beginning:

'I have now come out of the house and the door has been firmly shut. What an amazing experience! I definitely saw . . .'

The first part of your report will be in the present tense, the second in the past tense. Which gives the better sense of excitement, of your really being there?

## Choose the verb

Here are two accounts of the same incident.

ANN  I was walking behind Carol to the form room and she slammed the door on me. I unfortunately caught Carol in the eye with my hand as I tried to stop the door hitting me.

CAROL  I didn't know Ann was behind me so I closed the door after me. Next thing I knew, she smashed me in the eye with her fist.

Carol says she *closed* the door; Ann says she *slammed* it. Ann says she *caught* Carol's eye; Carol says Ann *smashed* it. Why have the girls chosen different verbs to describe the same thing?

Here are some verbs that all mean *looked*:

peeped   stared   glared   glanced.

Which would you use to show:
A  an amazed look?
B  a quick look?
C  an angry look?
D  a frightened look?


Now read this conversation.

'Jenkins, what are you smirking at?'
'I wasn't smirking, sir. I was just smiling.'
'You were smirking. You were grinning in your sarcastic way.'
'It was just a friendly smile, sir.'
'Stop that! Who did it? Who sniggered? Was it you, Brown?'
'No, sir. I chuckled a bit. That's all.'
'It was a nasty snigger. Jenkins, how dare you.'
'What, sir?'
'Guffaw like that in my lesson.'
'I was only laughing, sir. I thought it was funny.'

▭ There are six verbs connected with laughing in this piece of conversation. Pick them out. Make a dictionary definition for each one, giving in each case the shade of meaning it has. For example, one could be:

'laughing in a rude and noisy way'

Which one would this suit?
Look them up afterwards to see how near you were to the real meaning.

▭ Fill in the gap in each of these sentences with one of the two verbs that are in brackets after it. Use the verb that best fits the sentence.

1  The games teacher . . . around looking for trouble. (strolls, prowls)
2  Aziz . . . the ruler and angrily broke it in two. (snatched, took)
3  The Headmistress . . . the culprit to report to her at break. (told, ordered)
4  The force of the blow . . . the door off its hinges. (wrenched, pulled)
5  The vicar . . . the bride's hand. (grabbed, took)
6  The Queen . . . with joy when her son was saved. (cried, howled)

Check that you have chosen the same verbs as others in your group. Discuss why the ones you have chosen are right.

Most people know more words than they use. For instance, how many words do you know for *speaking*? Add to this list:

speak, say, whisper, yell, plead . . .

But most people when writing use only *says* or *said*.

▭ Imagine that you are watching a marathon. How many words do you know for *running*?

REMEMBER: If you use all the words you know you can make your meaning clearer. You will, therefore, write better.
Don't forget what you learned about using your thesaurus in *Book 1*.

# Mr Willow teaches the comma

'Right, today I'm going to teach you about using commas. That's the first use. Have you got it?'

'Well, Sir . . .'

'Very good, Adeole. You use it after a pausing word at the beginning of a sentence. I used one after *Right* and Adeole used one after *Well*. Now then, (that was another by the way) the second use is to mark off the person you're speaking to. Notice that I put one in front of *Adeole*. Wake up, you lot at the back! You're not listening. Did you notice I put one in front of *you lot at the back*? It doesn't have to be a proper noun does it, Andrew? It marks off whatever you call a person. Doesn't it, you idiot? See! I did it again.'

'Next there's using commas to mark off items in a list. Now tell me Adeole, Andrew, Jane, Benazir, Michelle and Joel, what am I using you as an example of?'

'People who are not listening, Sir.'

'No, you blethering idiots! You're items in a list.'

'We're not items, Sir. Not like apples, pears, bananas, cherries and peaches.'

'You're a list. So you need commas just the same. Got it?'

'Now this is an important one. Using commas like brackets to mark off the less important parts of a sentence. Here's an example. The teacher, a very kind man, gave the class no homework for a month. Now, why have I bracketed off *a very kind man*, Steven?'

'Because it must be a lie, Sir.'

'OK, smart guy, try this one for size. At break, when I see him, I'm going to ask the Headmaster to murder you. Now, which is the main part of the sentence as far as you're concerned?'

'When I see him, Sir.'

'No, you fool, that's the unimportant part I've bracketed off with commas.'

'Not really, Sir. I've just seen him going off in his car.'

'Right, that's it. I've had enough. You can teach yourselves. I'm off, while I'm still sane, to the staffroom. You lot, if you know what's good for you, will keep as quiet as mice. Next lesson, whenever that is, we'll do colons. That, as usual, will be another disaster. I've been in this school, I think, about twenty years. I've never, in all that time, met a class like you. I don't suppose, by the way, that one of you has noticed that I've been bracketing off the less important parts of my last few sentences with commas. I bet not one of you, you useless lot, can tell me when to use a comma.'

'At primary school I was told to use them when you paused, Sir.'

'Well, you're not at primary school now, Beth. You need to know more about them than that.'

Beth is partly right. The advice to use a comma when the reader needs to pause, is still good in secondary school. But Mr Willow has a point as well. It is helpful if you know the basic rules for the use of commas.

⇨ Make a list of rules setting out the use of commas, based on Mr Willow's speech. State each use and give two examples.

# FOOTNOTE

Sentences can be in the form of:

*statements*: He must have escaped.
*questions*: Where is he?
*exclamations*: Help!

Look at 'Danny's Nanny' on page 114. How many of each of these are there in 'Danny's Nanny'?
Look at the first page of 'Equal Rights' (page 100). How many statements, questions, and exclamations are there?
Why are there so many exclamations in comics?
Do you agree with Mr Willow (page 22) that they are mis-used?

# SPELL WELL

happiest    countries    poppies    sunniest

heard   learnt (no apostrophe in this word!)
earnings  fearful

something  someone  sometime  handsome

## 8

# DIALECT AND STANDARD ENGLISH

English would be easier if we all spoke the same, but we don't. We all speak a dialect, depending on the region we come from and where we live. This Step takes a further look at dialect and accent.
It leads to looking at the sentence again.

## A dialect fairy tale

Read 'Tom Tit Tot'.
This is how a familiar fairy tale was told in Suffolk. You may know it by another name.

### Tom Tit Tot

Well, once upon a time there were a woman, and she baked five pies. And when they come out of the oven they was that overbaked, the crust were too hard to eat. So she says to her darter:

   'Maw're,' says she, 'put you them there pies on the shelf an' leave them a little, an' they'll come agin.' – She meant, you know, the crust 'ud get soft.

But the gal, she says to herself, 'Well, if they'll come agin, I'll ate 'em now.' And she set to work and ate 'em all, first and last.

Well, come supper time the woman she said: 'Goo you and git one o' them there pies. I dare say they've come agin now.'

The gal she went an' she looked, an' there warn't nothn' but the dishes. So back she come, an' says she, 'Noo, they ain't come agin.'

'Not none o' them?' says the mother.

'Not none o' them,' says she.

'Well, come agin, or not come agin,' says the woman, 'I'll ha' one for supper.'

'But you can't if they ain't come,' says the gal.

'But I can,' says she. 'Goo you and bring the best of 'em.'

'Best or worst,' says the gal, 'I've ate 'em all, an' you can't ha' one till that's come agin.'

Well, the woman she were wholly bate, an' she took her spinnin' to the door to spin, and as she spun she sang:

'My darter ha' ate five, five pies to-day.
My darter ha' ate five, five pies to-day.'

The King, he were a' comin' down the street an' he hard her sing, but what she sang he couldn't hear, so he stopped and said,

'What were that you was a singin' of, maw'r?'

The woman, she were ashamed to let him hare what her darter had been a doin', so she sang, 'stids o' that:

'My darter ha' spun five, five skeins to-day.
My darter ha' spun five, five skeins to-day.'

'S'ars o' mine!' says the King, 'I never heerd tell o' anyone as could do that.'

Then he said: 'Look you here, I want a wife and I'll marry your darter. But look you here,' says he, ''leven months out o' the year she shall have all the vittles she likes to eat, and all the gownds she likes to git, an' all the cump'ny she likes to hev; but the last month o' the year she'll ha' to spin five skeins ev'ry day, an' if she doon't, I shall kill her.'

'All right,' says the woman, for she thowt what a grand marriage there was. And as for them five skeins, when te come tew, there'd be plenty o' ways o' gettin' out of it, and likeliest, he'd ha' forgot about it.

Well, so they was married. An' for 'leven months the gal had all the vittles she liked to ate, and all the gownds she liked to git, and all the cump'ny she liked to hev. But when the time was over she began to think about them there skeins an' to wonder if he had 'em in mind. But not one word did he say about 'em, an' she wholly thowt he'd forgot 'em.

Howsivir, the last day o' the last month, he takes her to a room she'd niver set eyes on afore. There warn't nothin' in it but a spinnin' wheel an' a stool. An', say he, 'Now me dear, hare you'll be shut in tomorrow with some vittles and some flax, and if you hain't spun five skeins by the night, yar hid'll goo off.'

An' away he went about his business. Well, she were that frightened. She'd allus been such a gatless mawther, that she didn't so much as know how to spin, an' what were she to dew tomorrer, with no one to come nigh to help her? She sat down on a stool in the kitchen, an' lork! how she did cry!

Howsivir, all on a sudden she hard a sort o' knockin' low down on the door. She upped and oped it, an' what should she see but a small little black thing with a long tail. That looked up at her right kewrious, an' that said:

'What are yew cryin' for?'

'What's that to yew?' says she.

'Nivir yew mind,' that said. 'But tell me what you're cryin' for?'

'That oon't dew me noo good if I dew,' says she.

'You doon't know that,' that said, an' twirled that's tail round.

'Well,' says she, 'that oon't dew no harm, if that doon't dew no good,' and she upped an' she told about the pies an' the skeins an' everything.

'This is what I'll do,' says the little black thing. 'I'll come to yar winder iv'ry mornin' an' take the flax an' bring it spun at night.'

'What's your pay?' says she.

That looked out o' the corners o' that's eyes an' said: I'll give you three guesses every night to guess my name, an' if you hain't guessed it afore the month's up, yew shall be mine.'

Well, she thowt she'd be sure to guess that's name afore the month was up. 'All right,' says she, 'I agree.'

'All right,' says that, an' lork! how that twirled that's tail!

Well, the next day, har husband he took har into the room, an' there was the flax an' the day's vittles.

'Now there's the flax,' says he, 'an' if that ain't spun up this night off goo yar hid!' An' then he went out an' locked the door.

He'd hardly gone, when there was a knockin' agin the winder. She upped and she oped it, an' there sure enough was the little oo'd thing a settin' on the ledge.

'Where's the flax?' says he.

'Here te be,' says she. And she gonned it to him.

Well, come the evenin', a knockin' come agin to the winder. She upped and she oped it and there was the little oo'd thing with five skeins of flax on his arm.

'Here to be,' says he, and he gonned it to her. 'Now what's my name?' says he.

'What, is that Bill?' says she.

'Noo, that ain't,' says he. An' he twirled his tail.

'Well, is that Ned?' says she.

'Noo, that ain't,' says he. An' he twirled his tail.

'Well, is that Mark?' says she.

'Noo, that ain't,' says he. And he twirled harder, an' awa' he flew.

Well, har husband he come in, there was the five skeins riddy for him. 'I see I shan't hev for to kill you to-night, me dare,' says he. 'Yew'll hev yar vittles and yar flax in the mornin',' says he, an' awa' he goes.

Well, ivery day the flax and the vittles, they was brought, an' ivery day that there little black impet used to come mornins and evenins. An' all the day the mawther she set a tryin' fur to think o' names to say to it when te come at night. But she niver hit on the right one. An' as that got to-warts the ind o' the month, the impet that began to look soo maliceful, an' that twirled that's tail faster an' faster each time she gave a guess.

At last te come to the last day but one. The impet that come along o' the five skeins an' that said:

'What, hain't yew got my name yet?'

'Is that Nicodemus?' says she.

'Noo, t'ain't,' that says.

'Is that Sammle?' says she.

'Noo, t'ain't,' that says.

'A-well, is that Methusalem?' says she.

'Noo, t'ain't that norther,' he says.

Then that looks at her with that's eyes like a cool o' fire, an' that says: 'Woman, there's only tomorrer night, and then yar'll be mine!' An' away that flew.

Well, she felt that horrud. Howsomediver, she hard the King a comin' along the passage. In he came, an' when he see the five skeins, he says, says he:

'Well my dare,' says he, 'I don't see but what you'll ha' your skeins riddy tomorrer night as well, an' as I reckon I shan't ha' to kill you, I'll ha' supper in here tonight.' So they brought supper an' another stool for him, and down the tew they set.

Well, he hadn't but a mouthful or so, when he stops an' begins to laugh.

'What is it?' says she.

'A-why,' says he, 'I was out a huntin' to-day, an' I got awa' to a place in the wood I'd never seen afore. An' there was an' ol' chalk pit. An' I heerd a sort o' a hummin', kind o'. So I got off my hobby, and went right quiet to the pit, an' I looked down. Well, what should be there but the funniest little black thing yew iver set eyes on. An' what was that dewin' on, but that had a little spinnin' wheel, an' that were spinnin' wonnerful fast, an' twirlin' that's tail. An' as that span that sang:

> 'Nimmy nimmy not
> My name's Tom Tit Tot.'

Well, when the mawther heerd this, she fared as if she could ha' jumped outer her skin for joy, but she didn't say a word.

Next day, that there little thing looked soo maliceful when he come for the flax. An' when night come, she heerd that a knockin' agin the winder panes. She oped the winder, an' that came right in on the ledge. That were grinnin'

from are to are, an' Oo! that's tail were twirlin' round that fast!

'What's my name?' that says, as that gonned har the skeins.

'Is that Solomon?' she says, pretendin' to be afeared.

'Noo, t'ain't,' that says, an' that come fudder into the room.

'Well, is that Zebedee?' says she again.

'Noo, t'ain't,' says the impet. An' then that laughed an' twirled that's tail till yew cou'n't hardly see it.

'Take time, woman,' that says; 'next guess *an' you'll be mine.*' An' that stretched out that's black hands at her.

Well, she backed a step or two, an' she looked at it, and then she laughed out, and says she, a pointin' of her finger at it,

> 'Nimmy nimmy not,
> Yar name's Tom Tit Tot!'

Well, when that hard her, that shruck awful, an' awa' that flew into the dark, an' she niver saw it noo more.

⊏⊐ Did you understand the dialect? What do each of these sentences from the story mean?

1 Well, the woman she were wholly bate.
2 I never heerd tell o' anyone as could do that.
3 She shall have all the vittles she likes to eat and all the gownds she likes to git.
4 She began to think about them there skeins an' to wonder if she had 'em in mind.
5 She'd allus been such a gatless mawther that she didn't so much know as how to spin, an' what were she to dew tomorrer with no one to come nigh to help her?
6 She upped and she oped it an' there sure enough was the little oo'd thing a settin' on the ledge.
7 'Here te be!' says she. And she gonned it to him.
8 So I got off my hobby, and went right quiet to the pit, an' I looked down.

⊏⊐ In small groups, decide whether the story would be better in normal (**Standard**) **English**. What are the advantages of the dialect form?

## Received Pronunciation

Of course, not everything would sound right in a local dialect. Read this, for instance:

**Here is the news. In Parliament today the Leader of the Opposition told the Prime Minister that she'd allus been a gatless mawther and she didn't know as how to run a bath let alone a country. Well, the Prime Minister she were wholly bate, and she upped and she gonned it to him proper.**

This wouldn't sound right, even in Suffolk. Why not?
A newsreader would read the news in Standard English which is called *Received Pronunciation* (RP). This is a southern dialect but the theory is that it is understood by more people than say a Geordie accent would be.
Which accent do you prefer? Are there some jobs where only RP is an accepted way of speech?

## Your own local story

Do you know any old stories about your own area? There are bound to be some ghost stories or tales about unusual people. Or perhaps there is a story about some unusual event in your family.

▷ Try to write down a story in your local dialect. Then tell each other your stories in your local accent.

# ASSESSMENT

Prepare a Record Sheet on your story like the one on page 16. Did you find it difficult to write in dialect?

# Agreement – the subject and the verb

Look at these sentences from 'Tom Tit Tot':

The pies was that overbaked.
They was married.
The girl were that frightened.

The Standard English versions would be:

The pies *were* so overbaked.
They *were* married.
The girl *was* frightened.

The verb word has been changed in each case.

The sentences could, though, be re-written:

The *pie* was so overbaked.
*She* was married.
The *girls* were frightened.

In these cases the main noun or pronoun in the sentence has been changed. Notice also that the verb is *to be* in all of the sentences. There clearly is a connection between the main noun (or pronoun) in a sentence and the verb form of *to be*.

## Singular and plural with the verb 'to be'

The main noun or pronoun in a sentence is called the **subject** of a sentence. The subject of a sentence controls the verb. If a subject is **plural** (more than one) the verb *to be* has to be in its plural form as well. This is why 'The pies *was* ...' is wrong. It should be 'The pies *were* ...'
If a subject is **singular** (only one) the verb *to be* has to be in its singular form. This is why 'The girl *were* ...' is wrong. It should be 'The girl *was* ...'

## Finding the subject

How do you find the subject of a sentence? You ask the question *Who?* or the question *What?* Put this question word in front of the verb. For example:

The girls played hockey.

The verb is *played*. You ask *Who played?* *The girls* is the answer; it is the subject of the sentence.

▭ Make up sentences using these verbs. Then put *Who?* or *What?* in front of the verb so that you can find the subject of your sentence. Underline the subject.

   went
   pushed
   runs
   ate
   jumped
   knitted

▭ Write your own sentences using these subjects:

   She
   The King
   Tom Tit Tot
   The mother
   The Prime Minister

## Singular and plural with the present tense

▭ From this passage pick out the verbs and then find their subjects. Some of the subjects will be pronouns because a pronoun can always take the place of a noun.

The horses galloped across the open field. They stopped at the fence. Desai climbed the fence. He held the bridle behind his back. The white mare spotted it. She reared up. She neighed loudly. The horses turned. They trotted away. Desai hesitated. Then he walked slowly home. His mother usually caught the horses. He would wait for her.

This passage is in the past tense. None of the verbs in this passage change whether the subject word is singular or plural.

The sentences below do need correcting because subject and verb don't match – there is no **agreement** (the technical word) between them. Notice that the sentences are in the present tense.

The river flow through the meadow.
We knows all the answers.
I thinks you drives well.
Samantha and Jane paints awful pictures.
The kitten play by the fire.

▭ Correct the sentences above.

Sometimes there can be a choice. We can say:

Liverpool is a good team. *or*
Liverpool are a good team.

Strictly speaking a team is singular, but we can think of it as eleven players and put it in the plural.

# FOOTNOTE  SPELL WELL

The subject and verb must agree:

1 When you are using the verb *to be*:

 The girls were going to university.
 The girl was going to university.

2 When you are using the *present tense*:

 The babies cry all the time.
 The baby cries all the time.

surplus   surreal   surface   measure

loss   bossy   floss   mossy

estate   loneliest   happiest   festival

# PLAY
# MAKING

## 9

Speech is looked at again in this Step. Plays are the most popular form of writing with teenagers, and, of course, they are mainly speech. This Step gives you more ideas and guidance on writing plays.
You may want to write a play in a dialect.

## Help in writing your plays

Look at these four pictures.

⫸ How do you know they are all pictures of people in plays? Discuss this in small groups.

1

2

3

4

## Putting in the words

⟹ Imagine what the people are saying to each other in the plays. Write down four lines of *dialogue* for each picture. Give each character a name. Set out your lines like this:

*Picture 1*

| | |
|---|---|
| CLARENCE | Have you heard the joke about the wide-mouthed frog? |
| GERTRUDE | Yes, you told me it five minutes ago. |
| CLARENCE | Well, there was this wide-mouthed frog, see . . . |
| GERTRUDE | Don't you ever listen to anything you're told? |

Decide what is happening in each picture before you write your lines.
Read out your lines to the rest of the group. Who has written the best ones? Read out the best ones of your group to the class.

## What shall I write a play about?

This question is often asked by pupils. One solution is to look in newspapers. You will find several things in there of interest to the playwright:

1 *Modern issues*
   A modern issue could be a thing like pollution. You could write about some children who set out to save North Sea seals and have an adventure.

2 *Heart-rending problems people and families suffer*
   A heart-rending problem could be about a family who are about to be turned out of their house. What can be done for them?

3 *Unusual stories*
   An unusual story might be one about a man who fell asleep in a skip and woke up to find himself on the way to the crusher.

No matter what your subject is, you will need to decide on how many scenes to write. Number 1 might be done like this:

SCENE ONE: Some children read of the seals' plight.
SCENE TWO: They set off to the beach – they could have an adventure on the way like being chased by a bull in a field.
SCENE THREE: They find a sick seal and decide to get it home on an old wheelbarrow they have found.
SCENE FOUR: They call in a vet. He tells them there is little chance but he does what he can.
SCENE FIVE: They keep the seal in the bath – family problems – and nurse it back to health.
SCENE SIX: They let it free again in the sea.

REMEMBER: Before you begin your play, write down each scene and briefly note what will be taking place.

## Cliff-hangers

It is sometimes important to end a scene by making the audience want to see what happens next. Note how the soaps on television often end a scene in this way. Where it is an extreme ending, like someone hanging on the edge of a tall building as the villain of the piece stamps on his or her fingers, it is known as a cliff-hanger. In the television soaps it is normally a bit of gossip or A upsetting B. Look at the ending of this scene:

(Janet and John are eloping in the middle of the night. John has put a ladder up to her bedroom window and has climbed up.)

JOHN    (Knocking) The ladder's secure, Janet.

JANET    Sh! Don't speak so loudly.

JOHN    (Assisting her) My darling!

JANET    In a few hours we will be married and hang to my father.

JOHN    Careful, darling.

(Cut to Janet's father and mother in bed)

FATHER    Did you hear a noise?

MOTHER    Yes, is it burglars?

FATHER    Where's my gun? I'll go and investigate.

(End of scene)

This scene does not tell you what happens. That is left till the next scene or episode. But it does make you want to know what *is going* to happen.

▭▷ Here are some cliff-hangers for you to write:

1 A and B are happily motoring through the Alps on holiday. They are going down a pass when the brakes fail.

2 A and B are talking about C on the telephone. They are being really insulting. C picks up her telephone and overhears part of the conversation on a crossed line. She gradually realises it is about her and she sets off to see A.

3 A and B are robbing a safe and saying how easy it has been to break in. Cut to safe owner who is telling his wife that he has planted a small explosive charge in the safe that will blow it up if the safe is not opened by the secret combination number. Back to the robbers forcing the door off.

4 A and B have not done their homework. They know that they can copy it from C. Cut to C. He has lost his homework book and is planning to copy the work from A. They meet in the classroom and discover not one of the three has done it. Teacher D who is really strict comes in.

5 A looks pale on board an aeroplane. He expresses his fear of flying to B. B tries to reassure him saying that flying is safer than travelling by car. Then the stewardess comes through from the pilot to announce an engine problem.

6 A's mother tells him he mustn't go out with B again. A argues but to no avail. Then through the window we see B's mother approaching.

## Language in plays

➡ Sometimes it's what we say; sometimes it's what we don't say; sometimes it's what we half-say. How true to life can you make the following situations? If improvisation in pairs helps, do this before you write the dialogues. Write five altogether (three from numbers 1–10; two from numbers 11–15).

1 Write at least ten lines of a play in which A persuades B to do something.
2 Write at least ten lines of a play in which A tells-off B.
3 Write at least ten lines of a play in which A suspects B of not telling the truth.
4 Write at least ten lines of a play in which A tries to find out a secret B is keeping hidden.
5 Write at least ten lines of a play in which A shows off to B who doesn't much care.
6 Write at least ten lines of a play in which A is the servant and B is the master.
7 Write at least ten lines of a play in which A shows he does not approve of B.
8 Write at least ten lines of a play in which A knows something damaging about B but does not say it outright.
9 Write at least twenty lines of a play in which A questions B closely about a crime.
10 Write at least fifteen lines of a play in which A is a headmaster or headmistress speaking to a school at assembly.
11 Write at least ten lines of a play in which A is the doctor and B is the patient (this could be serious or funny).
12 Write about twenty lines of a play in which A jokes about a situation or accident and B takes it seriously.
13 Write at least twenty lines of a play in which A exaggerates an experience to B who is not sure whether to believe him or her.
14 Write at least twenty lines of a play in which A makes up a story to try and fool B who is a teacher.
15 Write at least twenty lines of a play in which both A and B are very frightened.

You may like to develop some of these into a full scene or even a full play.

# Plays to complete

On pages 70–72 there are the beginnings of five scenes or situations on which plays could be developed. They are all realistic situations – things that could happen in real life.

▭ To begin with, work in pairs. Discuss your ideas and begin to plan out your plays scene by scene.

If you do improvisation in your classroom you might like to try improvising one or two of the ideas and then scripting down some or all of your improvisation. Some playwrights work in this way with groups of actors.

Then, on your own, write two plays. You can use any ideas presented here or come up with completely new ideas, if you like.

### SCENE: A classroom

| | |
|---|---|
| TEACHER | And where's yours, Alan? |
| ALAN | I've lost my file, Miss. |
| TEACHER | Which file? |
| ALAN | The literature one. |
| TEACHER | Where have you lost it? |
| ALAN | I don't know. |
| TEACHER | You didn't lend it to Samantha? |
| SAMANTHA | He didn't. Why pick on me? I'm always picked on. |
| TEACHER | Well, we all remember what happened last time. |
| SAMANTHA | That wasn't my fault. |
| TEACHER | Why didn't you do the homework on paper, Alan? |
| ALAN | I didn't have any. |

▭ Complete this scene or make it into a full play.

Discuss: What is the problem with Alan and his homework? Has someone else lost it and is Alan shielding them? How cross does the teacher get? Who else in the class is involved? Is the Head of Year called in? What is Alan or somebody else doing when the homework should be done? Are his parents called in? Schools are full of drama.

Other possible scenes: Head of Year's study; Alan's home; Outside school.

### SCENE: At home

| | |
|---|---|
| MOTHER | What time do you call this? |
| GIRL | I don't know. |
| MOTHER | Of course you know. |
| GIRL | Well, I'm just a bit late. |
| MOTHER | Just a bit! It's half-past-nine. |
| GIRL | All my mates stay out till ten. |
| MOTHER | I don't care about your mates. |
| FATHER | (Coming in) She's back is she. |
| MOTHER | Yes. |
| FATHER | You'll send me grey. |
| GIRL | I don't know why you worry. |
| FATHER | I worry because you're young and it's dark out there. So in future . . . |

▭ Complete this scene or make it into a full play.

Discuss: How can the problem be resolved? Are the parents old-fashioned or is the daughter unreasonable? Is it just one big row or do the family discuss it calmly? Rows make good drama. There could be a brother who is allowed in later which complicates things. A grandparent could get involved. The girl could defy her parents again and get into trouble.

SCENE: A school playground

A  You are small.

B  I can't help it.

A  No wonder you're called Titch. Half a titch would be better. Ha! Ha! Half a titch.

B  Don't.

A  Look, I've a proposition to put to you. You bring me 10p a day and I'll be your protector. I'll see no one bashes you up. There's a lot of bullying in this school. I'll protect you from it. What a bargain, just 10p. See you tomorrow. Keep this arrangement to yourself. No teachers to know. See! (Goes)

C  Has she been bullying you?

B  No.

C  Yes, she has. She wants money, doesn't she.

B  I can't say . . .

▭ Complete this scene or make a full play out of it.

Discuss: What can you call this play? Give names to A, B and C. What happens to B? Does A get her comeuppance? Are the teachers involved? Are parents involved? It would make a better play if the children solved the problem themselves without violence.

Other possible scenes: Outside school; B's home; A classroom.

SCENE: A wood

A  Look, if you climb up that tree you can swing across on that branch over to that other tree.

B  You show me then.

C  That stream's over six feet deep and it's fast flowing. If you fall in you could drown.

A  Scared of a bit of water. You can swim, can't you?

C  Not in that; you could get washed away.

A  Chicken!

B  He's not chicken.

A  Yes, he is. He never does anything we do. He's chicken . . .

▭ Complete this scene or make a full play out of this.

Discuss: What names would you give to A, B and C? What are the characters of A and C? What kind of daring things do A and B do? It would be interesting if A fell in and was rescued by C who becomes a hero.

Other possible scenes: A hospital; A's home. C's home.

**SCENE:** A school playground

A  Look what I've got in this box.
B  Give it me.
A  No, I'll hold it.
B  A spider! Cor, what a big one. What you got it in a box for?
A  You know how C can't stand spiders. I'm going to put it in his sandwich box.
B  He'll die!
A  I know. We all sit round getting out our dinner and then ... It'll be a hoot.
C  (Approaching) What you two doing?
A  Nothing.

⟹ Complete the scene or make a full play out of this.

Discuss: What are the names of A, B, and C? How does C react to the trick? Most people have a fear of something. What other plays could you write about fears? How can C get his own back? What could A's fear be?

Other possible scenes: In school; Headmistress's study; a night scene.

*ASSESSMENT*

Prepare a Record Sheet on the progress of your play writing.

# ARGUING IT OUT

## 10

Plays are full of argument between characters. But how well can you argue in speech and writing? Can you argue logically? This Step will help you.

'Oh, yes, he did!'
'Oh, no, he didn't!'
'Oh, yes, he did!'
'Oh, no, he didn't!'

This may be fine for a pantomine, but it isn't a sensible argument.
If an **argument** isn't to deteriorate into a *Yes, No* kind of confrontation, the people arguing must give reasons for their opinions, remain calm and avoid exaggerating their points.

⟹ Each of these statements is an exaggeration. Rewrite them so that they are reasonable statements.

1 British rivers are polluted – nothing can live in them.
2 It's always young people who cause trouble at football matches.
3 People buy only paperback books nowadays.

# Arguing logically

If you want to know why dogs are horrible, you've only got to look at my neighbour's. It tries to bite everyone it sees.

What is wrong with this argument?

⇨ Complete the following sentences by choosing the group of words, from the list below, which you think provides the most likely and logical reason. In each set of possible reasons, one will not only be illogical but simply untrue. Write it out and say why it is untrue. Then briefly say why you have rejected the other two reasons.

A I don't like wearing slippers because:

1 they don't keep your feet dry.
2 mine have holes in them.
3 they make my feet hot and sweaty.
4. they always have silly bobbles on them.

B I like a light kept on in my bedroom all night because:

1 I'm frightened of the dark.
2 it doesn't use much electricity.
3 I can see to read.
4 it stops spiders getting into my room.

C Everyone should be made to eat apples because:

1 they taste nice.
2 they frighten doctors.
3 they are cheaper than pineapples.
4 they prevent tooth decay.

D People should not be allowed to keep polar bears as pets:

1 because they cost a lot to feed.
2 because they encourage burglars.
3 because they might attack people.
4 because they are too big to take to a vet. So all the bears would die.

Now read this interview (opposite) from *Early Times*.

## *Write a summary*

⇨ Summarise Peter Newell's argument against smacking children. Use about 50 words. You could do it in short numbered sentences. Remember:

1 You are not agreeing or disagreeing. You are simply giving his argument.
2 Some of the material in the interview is not relevant to your summary. For instance, that smacking still goes on in many schools might show that Peter Newell has still much to do, but it hasn't any relevance to his argument against smacking.

## *Do you agree?*

⇨ In small groups, discuss how far you agree with Mr Newell's arguments. He uses particular examples (the Swedish doctors). Is this fair? Why would a law against smacking children be difficult to enforce? Decide whether a law should be tried or not. What form should a law of this kind take? Try to write out one beginning:

'It will be an offence to . . .'

# Cracking down on smacking

Press Ganger Jonathan Shapiro, 12, from Hertfordshire, interviews Peter Newell, director of the new charity EPOCH campaigning for an end to grown-ups physically punishing their children.

COULD it be that in the very near future the dreaded 'smacked bottom' will be a thing of the past? This is what Peter Newell who runs the new national organisation EPOCH (End Physical Punishment of Children) hopes.

I met Mr Peter Newell at his offices in London recently and discussed his views on smacking children. He has worked for a long time in children's rights societies, but in April decided to start his own campaign and has also written a book on the subject. The reason he feels so strongly about smacking children is that, 'it seems illogical that adults cannot hit adults but adults can hit children'.

## Hitting children

I asked him whether he had suffered physical punishment himself as a child, with dreadful consequences, but this was not so:

'The only time I was ever physically punished by my parents was when I stood in wet paint and trampled all over the house,' replied Peter.

'My mother pulled my hair, although they did not think spanking was a good thing to do.'

I then asked out of sheer curiosity what effect smacking has on children. He knew this question was coming, and tried to answer it briefly!

## Violence

'The odd smack here and there has little effect. The only lesson the children learn is to use smacking on their younger relations or own children later on. Children who are smacked tend to have a violent attitude.'

I wanted to know whether children who became delinquents had been smacked frequently in their early years, and he thought they probably had.

Most parents think that if they smack their children they will not misbehave again, but is this so? 'Not really,' Peter responded. 'Two-thirds of mothers hit their children who are under one year old and they are just as likely to do what they were smacked for again.'

I thought that corporal punishment in schools had stopped ages ago, but I learnt the facts from Peter Newall. Corporal punishment has only been banned in state schools since 1987, and teachers in private schools are still able to cane their pupils. In Scotland instead of using the cane, they use a leather strap.

## Police help

But in a way it is impossible to enforce the anti-smacking law that Mr Newell wants because there will not be a policeman around every time a child is smacked. But nevertheless, EPOCH believes that if a child is naughty, the parents should talk it over with them and make them understand what they did wrong.

For 10 years, Sweden has had a law prohibiting the smacking of children, but why was this law passed? Peter revealed to me that 20 years ago, Sweden had the same views on smacking as England. Many books suggested that children should be smacked.

However, during the 1970s a small group of doctors realised that this was harmful. The occurrence which made Sweden change the law was when a father severely battered his four-year-old daughter. When the case went before the magistrates court, the father's defence was that, 'it was his parental right to do so'. The father was acquitted [let off].

I asked Peter Newell whether he thought Swedish children would grow up less violent than the British. 'It's hard to say yet, as the Swedes don't have accurate figures,' he replied.

## Full potential

EPOCH believes that children can only achieve their full potential when they are recognised as individual people with rights of their own.

They also believe that children who are hit by their parents learn that violent solutions are acceptable, and they are more likely in turn to hit their own children.

## *Children's rights societies*

⟹ In your groups, draft a children's rights charter. Set it out in as clear and simple a manner as you can. You might start with:

'The following are considered the rights of every child. These rights will be enforced by law.'

# LETTERS

## 11

You may want to argue logically in a letter. Letter writing is still a major means of communication between people, despite inventions like the telephone, the computer and the fax machine.

If you can write a good letter, it will help you in life.

## Get the content and style right

Why? What? What not? How?

Nowhere is it more important to get your content and style right than in a letter. A letter can get you a job, help you out of a difficult situation, make you a friend – or an enemy, if you don't get it right! Ask yourself:

1 *Why? What is my purpose in writing this letter?*

For instance, letters of complaint are often simply rude. If all you want is to feel better by telling someone off, this may be justified. But most of us want some help with our problem, and we ought to say calmly and clearly what is wrong and what we wish to be done.

2 *What? What not?*

What does the person who receives the letter need to know? What do they not need to know? Many letters contain information that is of no relevance to the matter between writer and receiver.

3 *How?*

Choose your words carefully. The wrong choice can cause offence when none was intended.

Here's a comical illustration of an acceptable style of letter used for the wrong purpose. In what situation would this letter be correct? Why is it completely wrong here?

3 Newlands Road
Ramsgate
Kent
Thursday

Dear Miss Whitfield

I wish to apply for the position of your boyfriend, which I believe is now vacant, following the dismissal of Mr. Y. Young, owing to his failure to keep an appointment with you outside the Granada Cinema on Friday, the 12th of June.

I am quite tall, with brown hair and blue eyes, of smart appearance, punctual, and in general good health. My hobbies are gardening, stamp-collecting and watching television. I have recently taken 6 GCSE's and have reason to expect my results will be favourable.

I have had ambitions to become a boyfriend with you for the past two years, and have studied your progress keenly. I have had previous experience of the position with Miss Jenkins and Miss Taylor and I enclose testimonials from them.

If you regard my application favourably, I would seek an early interview to discuss the position more fully.

Yours sincerely

N.P. Lambert

# Business letters

There are no rules for writing social letters to friends, but there are certain rules that we use when writing formal letters, especially business letters.

*Always include:*

1 Your address
2 The date
3 A salutation: *Dear Aziz, Dear Sirs, Dear Mrs Jones.*
4 A suitable subscription: *Yours sincerely* or *Yours faithfully.*
   NB: *Yours* begins with a capital letter but *sincerely* and *faithfully* do not.

*Remember:*

1 In a business or formal letter, if you give the person's name in the salutation for example, *Dear John* or *Dear Ms Jones* you should always close your letter *Yours sincerely.*
   If you are writing to an unknown person, for example, *Dear Sir* or *Dear Madam* then you should close your letter *Yours faithfully.*
2 It is not common practice to punctuate the address, the date, the salutation or the subscription (Yours etc . . .) in a business letter.
3 Letters between companies usually include a reference (usually in the form: *Your ref: account no. 1234*). This reference often makes all the difference between a quick reply and no reply at all. So you are well advised to use it when writing a reply to a company.
4 Write your business letter in short spaced out paragraphs as in N.P. Lambert's letter.

▭ Write the *testimonial* one of the girls sends to Miss Whitfield using the same tone and style of letter. You could begin:

'With reference to your enquiry about the character of Mr N.P. Lambert, I can supply the following confidential information . . .'

▭ Look at the following letters (pages 80–81) and make a list of the content and style that is not correct for the writer's purpose. Also note any detail that should have been included to make the writer's purpose clear.

*FOOTNOTE*

A testimonial should be written in formal language, like the letter on page 78. In a testimonial you write about a person's good points: their character, abilities and qualifications.

3 Anderson Terrace
Gosforth
Newcastle
8th December

Dear Sir

### Lost Handbag

I caught the 8.15 am. train from King's Cross on Thursday and had reached Peterborough, when I decided I'd try and finish my book: 'The Heart's Ease'. I started to rummage through my holdall and found it wasn't there. Then I remembered I'd put it in my handbag, but that wasn't there either. Then I remembered where I'd left it, my handbag I mean, with the book in it.

Anyway, it's on the counter of the buffet, in the corner of King's Cross station. It's probably not there now, because somebody will be sure to have nicked it, unless one of the staff put it under the counter for safety.

Luckily I was alright for money, because my purse wasn't in the handbag. What I'd done was pay for the cup of coffee and then put my purse back in my holdall before I'd put it in my handbag.

So, if you've found a red handbag in your lost property that's come from King's Cross it's probably mine. If you send it back, I'll pay the postage.

Yours sincerely

Evelina Maglongawe

Arthur Kennedy School
Acacia Avenue
Fulbridge

Dear Mrs King

### Bus Trip to Chessington Zoo

I wish to order a bus to take Form 5B to Chessington Zoo a week on Tuesday. Your secretary said it would cost £120 and that's OK by me, because I rang up Marshall's Super Coaches yesterday and they asked for one hundred and fifty quid which I reckon is a right rip-off.

We would like to start about eight o'clock, which will give the kids who live in the villages time to get in; but we'll have to go by Barkestone to pick up Mike Armitage because his dad's car's bust, and there's no way that clapped-out Barkestone bus is going to get Mike to school by eight.

We need to get back about ten at night and some people will have to be dropped off around the villages, because I can't see any other way they'll get home, unless they leg it, and I'll doubt they'll do that because they'll be half dead from trogging round the zoo all day. If this means we need to fork out a bit more dough, you'll have to let us know.

See you Tuesday

John Poynton

➡ Rewrite the last two letters in a style and with a content that is correct for their purpose.

➡ Then write *one* of the following letters:

1  a letter enquiring about tickets for a pop concert giving the different dates you can go;
2  a letter to the owner of the wallet you found who lives in the USA;
3  a letter to a charity worker inviting her to come to your school to give a talk.

ASSESSMENT

Prepare a Record Sheet of your progress in writing letters.

# IMPROVING YOUR WRITING

## 12

You might want to give someone a vivid account of a holiday in a letter. One way of doing this is to use similes.
We look at part of a very famous and colourful poem to see how a poet uses similes.
We also learn about clichés.

## Looking at a famous poem

The 'Ancient Mariner' (old sailor) in the poem that follows 'must' tell his story. He has to re-tell the terrible tale of what happened to him and his ship so that he can free himself from the guilt he still feels. He describes how he first felt this compulsion.

Forthwith this frame of mine was wrenched
With woeful agony,
Which forced me to begin my tale;
And then it left me free.

Since then, at an uncertain hour,
That agony returns;
And till my ghastly tale is told,
This heart within me burns.

I pass, like night, from land to land;
I have strange power of speech;
That moment that his face I see,
I know the man that must hear me:
To him my tale I teach.

At the beginning of this *narrative* (story) poem the ancient mariner has seen another face to whom he must tell his tale – it is one of a group of three men about to go to a wedding. Naturally the wedding guest does not want to hear, but he has to submit to the will of the old man – the need to tell his story is so strong. Here's how the poem begins:

# The Rime of the Ancient Mariner

## Part I

An ancient Mariner meeteth three Gallants bidden to a wedding-feast, and detaineth one.

It is an ancient Mariner
And he stoppeth one of three.
'By thy long grey beard and glittering eye,
Now wherefore stopp'st thou me?

The Bridegroom's doors are opened wide,
And I am next of kin;
The guests are met, the feast is set:
May'st hear the merry din.'

He holds him with his skinny hand,
'There was a ship,' quoth he.
'Hold off! unhand me, grey-beard loon!'
Eftsoons his hand dropt he.

The Wedding-Guest is spell-bound by the eye of the old seafaring man, and constrained to hear his tale.

He holds him with his glittering eye –
The Wedding-Guest stood still,
And listens like a three years' child:
The Mariner hath his will.

The Wedding-Guest sat on a stone:
He cannot choose but hear;
And thus spake on that ancient man;
The bright-eyed Mariner.

'The ship was cheered, the harbour cleared,
Merrily did we drop
Below the kirk, below the hill,
Below the lighthouse top.

The Mariner tells how the ship sailed southward with a good wind and fair weather, till it reached the Line.

The sun came up upon the left,
Out of the sea came he!
And he shone bright, and on the right
Went down into the sea.

Higher and higher every day,
Till over the mast at noon –'
The Wedding-Guest here beat his breast,
For he heard the loud bassoon.

The Wedding-Guest heareth the bridal music; but the Mariner continueth his tale.

The bride hath paced into the hall,
Red as a rose is she;
Nodding their heads before her goes
The merry minstrelsy.

The Wedding-Guest he beat his breast,
Yet he cannot choose but hear;
And thus spake on that ancient man,
The bright-eyed Mariner:

The ship driven by a storm toward the South Pole.

'And now the STORM-BLAST came, and he
Was tyrannous and strong:
He struck with his o'ertaking wings,
And chased us south along.

With sloping masts and dipping prow,
As who pursued with yell and blow
Still treads the shadow of his foe,
And forward bends his head,
The ship drove fast, loud roared the blast,
And southward aye we fled.

And now there came both mist and snow
And it grew wondrous cold:
And ice, mast-high, came floating by,
As green as emerald.

The land of ice, and of fearful sounds where no living thing was to be seen.

And through the drifts the snowy clifts
Did send a dismal sheen:
Nor shapes of men nor beasts we ken –
The ice was all between.

The ice was here, the ice was there,
The ice was all around:
It cracked and growled, and roared and howled,
Like noises in a swound!

Till a great sea-bird, called the Albatross, came through the snow-fog, and was received with great joy and hospitality.

At length did cross an Albatross,
Thorough the fog it came;
As if it had been a Christian soul,
We hailed it in God's name.

It ate the food it ne'er had eat,
And round and round it flew.
The ice did split with a thunder-fit;
The helmsman steered us through!

And lo! the Albatross proveth a bird of good omen, and followeth the ship as it returned northward through fog and floating ice.

And a good south wind sprung up behind;
The Albatross did follow,
And every day, for food or play,
Came to the mariners' hollo!

In mist or cloud, on mast or shroud,
It perched for vespers nine;
Whiles all the night, through fog-smoke white,
Glimmered the white moonshine.'

The ancient Mariner
inhospitably killeth the pious
bird of good omen.

'God save thee, ancient Mariner,
From the fiends that plague thee thus! –
Why look' st thou so?' – 'With my crossbow
I shot the ALBATROSS.

On the surface the old sailor does not seem
to have done anything wrong in shooting
the albatross, but remember:

1 The poem is set in the days of sailing
ships which relied on winds and were
vulnerable to storms.
2 The sea was a frightening place;
travellers always risked their lives. Many
did not return. Those that did brought
back strange tales of amazing lands and
peoples.
3 Sailors were naturally superstitious. Any
crisis could be blamed on the smallest
things – like shooting a friendly bird!

## Complete the tale

▭ Write your version (don't try verse) of
the ancient mariner's tale. It can be a real
or a supernatural one – you can make it
horrific. Whatever it was that happened to
the ship and crew, the story certainly
impressed the wedding-guest. After he had
heard the tale:

He went like one that hath been stunned,
And is of sense forlorn:
A sadder and a wiser man,
He woke the morrow morn.

# Similes

Look at these lines from 'The Ancient
Mariner'.

1 And listens like a three years' child

2 I fear thee, ancient Mariner!
I fear thy skinny hand!
And thou art long, and lank, and brown,
As is the ribbed sea-sand.

3 And ice, mast-high, came floating by,
As green as emerald.

4 As idle as a painted ship
Upon a painted ocean.

5 We could not speak, no more than if
We had been choked with soot.

6 The souls did from their bodies fly-
They fled to bliss or woe!
And every soul, it passed me by,
Like the whizz of my cross-bow.

▭ Answer these questions:

1 Which comparison (*simile*) gives us the
idea that the icebergs, though dangerous,
were striking and beautiful to look at?
2 Which gives us a vision of a completely
becalmed ship? How?
3 How does the poem express the idea of
mouths so parched that they couldn't
utter a sound?

4 Who 'listens like a three years' child'?
What does this show about the way he
was listening?
5 The ancient mariner's companions
dropped dead one by one. He imagines
he can hear their souls pass 'Like the
whizz of my cross-bow'. Why does this
comparison occur to the ancient
mariner?
6 Which simile describes the ancient
mariner? What is he compared to?

 FOOTNOTE

Similes are comparisons using *like* or *as*.
Similes help to give us a clearer idea of
what is happening, usually in the form of a
sight or experience we are familiar with.

# Clichés

One simile for the bride (Red as a rose is
she) has now been used so often it has lost
its force. Similes that no longer make us
think or respond are called *clichés*. Here
are some:

as soft as grease
as white as snow
as old as the hills
as green as grass
as heavy as lead
as plain as a pikestaff
as clear as mud
as easy as falling off a log
as swift as an arrow
as sick as a parrot
as smooth as silk
as deep as a well
as pretty as a picture
as big as a house
as bright as a button
as quiet as a mouse
as cold as charity
as alike as two peas in a pod

Some of these are still used although their
meanings are now obscure. Why *as plain
as a pikestaff*, for instance? Why should
*charity* be *cold*?
In speech it is difficult to avoid using
clichés. But where we have time, as in
writing, we can think up our own original
comparisons.

⊏⊐ Replace the above with new
comparisons. *Don't* fall into the trap of
replacing one cliché with another. Don't
use *as soft as butter*, for instance. In other
words, if you have heard the comparison
before, don't write it. Remember you live in
the 1990s, so be very modern. What is as
*swift as an arrow* today, for instance?
When you have done this on your own
meet in your groups to decide who has
written the most original. Then decide
which are the best in the class.

⇨ On your own, write a piece describing someone, using two or three similes. But before you do, look at Sally's description. She has just learned to do similes. Some of her comparisons are good (which do you like?) but there are far too many. The reader becomes confused.


## Claudia Spy

Claudia Spy is very tall and slim. She stands like a netball post, but she is not quite that slim. Her nose is like a peg sticking out from a face full of craters. Her ears are like the wings of a bird. Her eyes are sleek and slender, and stare at you like emeralds. Wherever you walk the eyes of Claudia Spy are on you. She knows when you are spying on her. Her vision is almost that of a cat. Her lips are like sticks of rock, with thick red lip-stick. Her teeth are like icicles inside a cave. Her hair sticks out like pieces of wire. Her fingers are like twigs, her long nails like daggers.

# THE WORLD OF ADVERTISING

## 13

Is the picture taking over from the written word? Many people today would rather watch television than read a book. Pictures can have a powerful effect, but if they are coupled with words, they can have an even more powerful effect. The advertisers know this and spend millions on putting the right words with the right pictures.

If you know something about it, you can arm yourself against the advertisers and their persuasions.

## Images

Look at the For Sale sign below. A hopeless advert, you might think – but an estate agent in London who used this kind of advertisement for some of his properties found it brought in more customers than the usual type of advert. Can you think why?

```
                        For Sale
                        ‾‾‾‾‾‾‾‾

Very small two-bedroomed house, parts of which need expensive
repairs, at the ridiculously high price of £40,000. Not really
worth looking at, and don't bring Long John Silver with you or
he may get woodworm in his wooden leg. But if you must, contact:

            LAWRENCE and CARTER
            92 Firsland Way
            Belton
            Tel: Belton 99731
```

⇨ Advertise your own house, bungalow or flat, or your school, or an old building near you in a similar manner.

Increasing competition to sell makes advertisers try an increasing number of methods to catch your attention. One of the favourites is to use a picture – an image – that catches your eye. There is often not an obvious connection between the picture and the advertisement. But you want to read the *advertising copy* (the words) because you want to work out the connection.

## Write your own advertising copy

⇨ Here are three advertisers' pictures without the words. Make up the copy for each one. Work out what you think each might be advertising, and write about four sentences for each, naming the product and connecting its virtues with the picture.

⇨ Bring in your own pictures taken from magazines and newspapers. Cut out the copy first (but save it) and ask other members of your group to write advertising copy for each picture. Compare these with the original copy you saved.

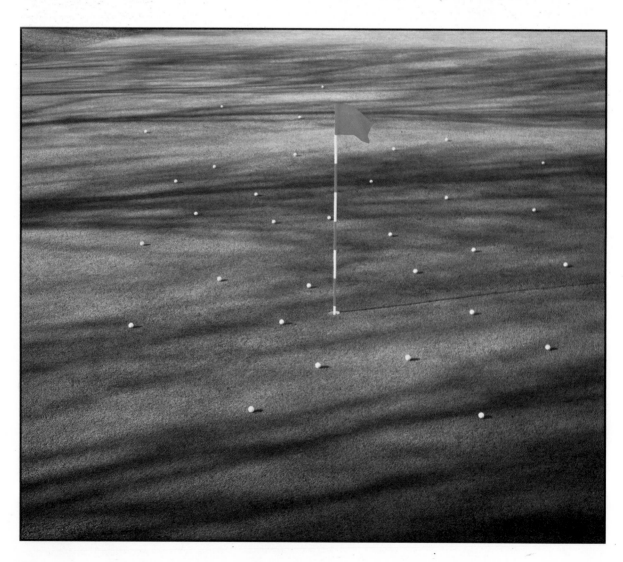

➡ Here are three more striking pictures that advertisers might use. Decide what you would use each to advertise, and write the copy.

Have a good discussion just as they would do in an advertising agency. If it is a product rather than a service you want to advertise, think up a list of names for the product and then decide on the best. In advertising, special people are employed just to think up names for a product.

## ASSESSMENT

Prepare a Record Sheet on your progress in writing advertising copy.

---

# THINGS THAT HAPPEN IN REAL LIFE

## 14

People who read a lot are usually good at English.
Here are two stories about things that happen in real life. As you grow older you will learn whether you prefer to read 'real' stories or 'fantasy' stories. You may have a real story to tell as well.
You will have a chance to do a book review and to revise direct and reported speech.

The best stories are often from direct personal experience – a detailed record of a happy or sad event from your own life.
In this first story there is not a great deal of **plot** but what happens to the boy is important. You do not need lots of things happening (plot) to make a good story if the writing has a true feel to it.
'The Visitor' was written by a Jamaican writer, H. Orlando Patterson. Pay attention to the way he uses dialect in the story. If there are any words you do not understand, look them up in your dictionary.

## The Visitor

He was odd. Below his grey, felt hat he had an uncertain smile which confused me a little as I somehow got the strange impression that I was making him uncomfortable. He remained silent for a long time. I began to detect something sinister about him.

Suddenly, he said, in an almost apologetic voice, 'You Miss Gladys' son?' There was a faint smell of rum and toothpaste. I nodded. He kept staring at me; his mouth remained slightly open. His eyes were watery, curious and a little sad.

'You want me to call her for you?' I asked.

'What?' He seemed surprised that I was capable of asking a question; or perhaps that I had been daring enough to put one to him. He swallowed, stared at me with even greater curiosity, and then murmured. 'Oh, call her? Yes, yes, do that.'

What a funny man, I thought, as I went to the door.

'Mamma.'

'What?'

'A man out here to see you.'

'A man? Which man that?'

'Don't know him. Never seen him before.'

She got up and peeped through the window. By now I was anxious myself to know who the stranger might be and so I observed her closely as she peered outside at him. She stared and stared. She did not move and seemed petrified by the window. I walked inside and had a mild shock as I saw her expression.

'What happen, Mamma?'

She did not answer. I realised that something was very wrong. I had never known her to be confronted with a situation which she seemed in any way incapable of handling. Not until that moment.

'Mamma . . . ?'

'Go an' tell 'im me not here . . . go an' tell 'im . . . no, wait, tell 'im . . . tell 'im me coming.'

Whoever the stranger was I realised that he somehow threatened us and instinctively began to fear him. Yet, when I walked back to him his appearance instilled little apprehension in me. His manner was uncertain, vague and distant. It reassured me against my every instinct. I even had, for a moment, the absurd impression that he was afraid of us. And this flattered my childhood pride.

'My mother says she coming,' I told him.

He said thanks softly. My mother walked out of the door, then stopped and continued to stare at him. He walked towards her and stopped a few yards away. A conspiracy of silence seemed to reign between them, between us I should say, for by now I too was left simply staring, wondering what it was all about. It was he who finally broke the silence.

'Hi, Gladys. I hope I didn't surprise you too much?'

'How you find where I live?' Her voice was unusually restrained, though there was an ever so slight note of threat in it.

'Oh, I was jus' passing through the town. I ask at the China-man shop if they know you, an' they show me the way . . . .'

After another long pause she beckoned to him to come inside. The door remained half-closed and I remained staring at it for the next fifteen minutes. Then I heard my mother calling me. My heart leapt at the thought of finally solving the mystery of the stranger. I found myself stuffing my shirt into my trousers respectfully. My mother called again, impatiently. I ran inside.

He was sitting on the only chair we had; she was on the edge of the bed. They both looked at me as I entered. I made sure to avoid his eyes, staring at her for refuge. Then after another long pause, she beckoned to him hesitantly and mumbled, 'Your father.'

I was a little surprised, of course, but not shocked. Perhaps more confused than anything else. I had known he existed somewhere in some shape. But my conception of him had been vague, formless. He had been part of my own personal folk-lore: something I had liked and at times dreamt about, like expensive gold-fish, but never really desired, never took quite seriously. Seeing him there before me, I was sure I would have been no less confounded had I been faced with Humpty-Dumpty. What could I say? What was I expected to say? They expected me to look at him. Well, I looked at him.

He had lines on his brow and his cheeks were rough. I thought he must shave every day; my friends had told me their fathers did. I thought it would have been very funny if my mother had had to shave every day too; I was not unconscious of my stupid notion.

He nodded in a gesture of approval as he stared at me.

'You are a fine boy,' he said; and I wondered what he meant. Then he looked at my mother and in the same uncertain, unconvincing voice, he repeated, 'He's a fine boy.'

My mother murmured something in response, then glanced at me. Her eyes lacked the proud gleam of satisfaction which it usually bore when someone flattered me in this manner. Instead, it was slightly censorious: I could detect a hint of anger in them and I felt lost to explain why she should have reacted in this manner. When she looked away she held down her head, and if I hadn't known her so well I would have been convinced that there was shame in her eyes. After that she rested her elbow on her knee and her chin between her fingers and sighed, which I knew, was her silent, physical way of repeating an expression that was always on her lips: 'Oh, what a life, my God!'

I kept wondering what was going on. I had observed adults to act in the strangest way before; but underlying my ignorance, there had always been some gleam of understanding, some awareness, if ever so remote, that whatever they were up to was somehow meaningful. But the behaviour of my mother and the stranger now completely baffled me. Why didn't they say something? Did they hate each other? Did the fact that he was my father mean all that much to her?

Suddenly, I was overwhelmed with the fear that he had come to take her away from me. Perhaps it was that which was worrying them. They did not know how to tell me. My mother would be leaving me all alone. In an instant, the essence of my relationship with her, the importance of her presence, impressed itself on me. I neither loved her nor hated her. I feared her a little, perhaps, for often she would beat me cruelly. But the rage I expressed then in my tears was purely an immediate reaction to the pain I felt. Somehow I conceived that beating me had meant far more to her than it had to me. The world was tough; so she often told me. I was her child and completely at her mercy; it was only natural. Despite everything, a strong bond held us together. Nothing positive, really; more the fear that if we lost each other we would have lost everything. For me she was the person I called mother; she gave me food, clothes and the books I read at school. And she taught me to be good. It was never quite clear what she meant by being good. More often than not, it simply meant *being good* to her, or not being ungrateful, which amounted to much the same thing. I suppose she could be said to have been warm in her own way. But unconsciously, she taught me not to expect very much and so I asked for very little. All I desired was for her to be there, always there. Now there was the threat of her departure.

But that was not possible. I reassured myself that I was being silly to the point of deciding that it would have been better if I left the room. Perhaps they wished to say adult things. As soon as I began to nudge my way to the door I heard him saying, in a manner which suggested that he was repeating himself, 'Yes, it's been a long time, Gladys.' I decided then that I was certainly the reason for their apparent discomfort, and I began to move less imperceptibly to the door. Suddenly I heard my mother call my name. Her voice was sharp and severe; she did not have to say that I must stay; her tone was enough.

The stranger looked at me quizzically, then back at her and suddenly sprang out of his chair. He made the usual motions which indicated an intention to depart; yet, he hesitated. Then he suddenly seemed to remember something. He took out a five-shilling note from his trouser pocket and handed it to me.

'Buy a present with it,' he said.

I stared at the note, a little shocked, both at the large sum of money and at the fact that he, of all people, should have given it to me. I looked up at my mother to see what her response was. I was not surprised when she said, 'Give it back.' Then she turned to him and said, 'I bring 'im up all this time without your help; I don't need it now.'

I immediately held the money out to him for I realised that my mother was in no mood to be crossed. I began to dread the moment when I would be alone with her.

The man began to protest, but he broke off suddenly and took back the note from me. I began to feel sorry for him, for he seemed insulted and sad. He took up his little felt hat, put it on his head and left without saying another word. I never saw him again.

H. Orlando Patterson

⊏⊐ In small groups, discuss the story.

1 Why does the boy think the man is 'odd' at the beginning of the story?
2 Why does the mother not want to see the man?
3 Why might the mother not be happy to be told that her son is 'a fine boy'?
4 What does the boy fear will happen when the mother and father remain silent?
5 Why is the boy made to give the money back?

The next story is a story to make you think – the best stories do this.

## Equal Rights

'Can't you read?'

The man was looking at me and reaching under the counter as if he was going for his gun. He came up with another one of his signs to spread over the front of a paper.

'"Only two children at a time allowed in this shop"', he read out, loudly.

I looked across at the two kids in the corner. They were pretending to pick Penny Chews while they gawped at the girls on the magazines. OK, I made three, but I wasn't there for the same reason as them. Couldn't he recognise business when he saw it?

'I'm not buying,' I said, 'I've come about the job.'

He frowned at me, in between watching the boys in the corner. 'What job?' he said. He was all on edge with three of us in the shop.

'"Reliable paper boy wanted"', I told him. '"Enquire within." It's in the window. I'm enquiring within.'

'Hurry up, you two!' he shouted. And then he frowned at me again as if I was something from outer space.

'But you're not a boy,' he said. '"Reliable paper *boy* required", that says. If I'd meant "boy *or girl*" I'd have put it on, wouldn't I? Or "paper *person*"!' He did this false laugh for the benefit of a man with a briefcase standing at the counter.

'Oh,' I said, disappointed. 'Only I'm *reliable*, that's all. I get up early with my

100

dad, I'm never off school, and I can tell the difference between the *Sun* and the *Beano*.'

    'I'm glad someone can,' the man with the briefcase said.

    But the paper man didn't laugh. He was looking at me, hard.

    'Where d'you live?' he asked.

    'Round the corner.'

    'Could you start at seven?'

'Six, if you like.'

'Rain or shine, winter and summer?'

'No problem.' I stared at him, and he stared at me. He looked as if he was deciding whether or not to give women the vote.

'All right,' he said, 'I'll give you a chance. Start Monday. Seven o'clock, do your own marking-up. Four pounds a week, plus Christmas tips. Two weeks' holiday without pay . . .'

Now that he'd made up his mind he smiled at me over-doing the big favour.

'Is that what the boys get?' I asked. 'Four pounds a week?'

He started unwrapping a packet of fags. 'I don't see how that concerns you. The money suits or it doesn't. Four pounds is what I said, and four pounds is what I meant. Take it or leave it.' He looked at Briefcase again, shaking his head at the cheek of the girl.

I walked back to the door. 'I'll leave it, then,' I said, 'seeing the boys get five pounds, *and* a week's holiday with pay.' I knew all this because Jason used to do it. 'Thanks anyway, I'll tell my dad what you said . . .'

'Please yourself.'

I slammed out of the shop. I was mad, I can tell you, Cheap labour, he was after: thought he was on to a good thing for a minute, you could tell that.

The trouble was, I really needed a bit of money coming in, saving for those shoes and things I wanted. There was no way I'd get them otherwise. But I wasn't going to be treated any different from the boys. I wouldn't have a shorter round or lighter papers, would I? Everything'd be the same, except the money.

I walked the long way home, thinking. It was nowhere near Guy Fawkes, and Carol Singing was even further away. So that really only left car washing – and they leave the rain to wash the cars round our way.

Hearing this baby cry gave me the idea. Without thinking about it I knocked at the door where the bawling was coming from.

The lady opened it and stared at me like you stare at double-glazing salesmen, when you're cross for being brought to the door.

'"Baby-play calling"', I said – making up the name from somewhere.

The lady said, 'Eh?' and she looked behind me to see who was pulling my strings.

'"Baby-play"', I said. 'We come and play with your baby in your own home. Keep it happy. Or walk it out – not going across main roads.'

She opened the door a bit wider. The baby crying got louder.

'How much?' she asked.

That really surprised me. I'd felt sorry about calling from the first lift of the knocker, and here she was taking me seriously.

'I don't know,' I said. 'Whatever you think . . .'

'Well . . .' She looked at me to see if she'd seen me before; to see if I was local enough to be trusted. Then I was glad I had the school jumper on, so she knew I could be traced. 'You push Bobby down the shops and get Mr

Dawson's magazines, and I'll give you twenty pence. Take your time, mind . . .'

'All right,' I said. 'Thank you very much.'

She got this little push-chair out, and the baby came as good as gold – put its foot in the wheel a couple of times and nearly twisted its head off trying to see who I was, but I kept up the talking, and I stopped while it stared out a cat, so there wasn't any fuss.

When I got to the paper shop I took Bobby in with me.

'Afternoon,' I said, trying not to make too much of coming back. 'We've come down for Mr Dawson's papers, haven't we, Bobby?'

You should have seen the man's face.

'Mr Dawson's?' he asked, burning his finger on a match. 'Number twenty-nine?'

'Yes, please.'

'Are you . . .?' He nodded at Bobby and then at me as if he was making some link between us.

'That's right,' I said.

He fumbled at a pile behind him and lifted out the magazines. He laid them on the counter.

'Dawson', it said on the top. I looked at the titles to see what Mr Dawson enjoyed reading.

*Workers' Rights* was one of them. And *Trade Union Times* was the other. They had pictures on their fronts. One had two men pulling together on a rope. The other had a woman bus-driver waving out of her little window. They told you the sort of man Mr Dawson was – one of those trade union people you get on television kicking up a fuss over wages, or getting cross when women are treated different to men. Just the sort of bloke I could do with on my side, I thought.

The man was still fiddling about with his pile of magazines.

'Oh, look,' he said, with a green grin. 'I've got last month's *Pop Today* left over. You can have it if you like, with my compliments . . .'

'Thanks a lot,' I said. Now I saw the link in his mind. He thought I was Mr Dawson's daughter. He thought there'd be all sorts of trouble now, over me being offered lower wages than the boys.

'And about that job. Stupid of me, I'd got it wrong. What did I say – *four* pounds a week?'

'I think so,' I said. 'It sounded like a four.'

'How daft can you get? It was those kids in the corner. Took my attention off. Of course it's *five*, you realise that. Have you spoken to your dad yet?'

'No, not yet.'

He stopped leaning so hard on the counter. 'Are you still interested?'

'Yes. Thank you very much.'

He came round the front and shook hands with me. 'Monday at seven,' he said. 'Don't be late . . .' But you could tell he was only saying it, pretending to be the big boss.

'Right.' I turned the push-chair round. 'Say ta-ta to the man, Bobby,' I said.
Bobby just stared, like at the cat.

The paper man leaned over. 'Dear little chap,' he said.

'Yeah, smashing. But Bobby's a girl, not a chap, aren't you, Bobby? At least, that's what Mrs Dawson just told me.'

I went out of the shop, while my new boss made this funny gurgling sound, and knocked a pile of papers on the floor.

He'd made a show-up of himself, found out too late that I wasn't Mr Dawson's daughter.

I ran and laughed and zig-zagged Bobby along the pavement. 'Good for us! Equal rights, eh, Bobby? Equal rights!'

But Bobby's mind was all on the ride. She couldn't care less what I was shouting. All she wanted was someone to push her fast, to feel the wind on her face. Boy or girl, it was all the same to her.

Bernard Ashley

▭ Discuss the story in small groups.

1 Do you think boys and girls are treated equally at home, in school, in the outside world?
2 Do you think children generally are given 'equal rights' with adults?
3 Give examples from your experience to show how you were discriminated against because you were young.
4 Are there times when adults and children should not have 'equal rights'?

## Write your own story

The girl in the story makes Mr Dawson change his mind. Write about a time when you have made someone change his or her mind, or when the same thing has been done to you. *Or* write about the most important event in your life.

## Write a book review

When you have read the two stories write a book review for each of them in which you:

1 write briefly about the plot without giving away the end.
2 say why or why not you liked the story.
3 say how true it is to real life.
4 say what you think about the style of the writing (Is it easy to read? Are the sentences too complicated?)
5 say what age group the story is suitable for.
6 say what mark you would give it out of ten.

## ASSESSMENT

Prepare a Record Sheet on your progress in writing a story and a book review.

- - - - - - - - - - - - - - - - -

# Conversation: direct speech

The stories are made more lively by the use of conversation. For example, in 'Equal Rights':

'Where do you live?' he asked.
'Round the corner.'
'Could you start at seven?'
'Six, if you like.'

This could have been written:

The paperman asked where she lived. She replied that she lived round the corner. He then asked her if she could start at seven. She said that she could start at six, if he liked.

Which of the above examples is direct speech? Which is reported speech?

▭▷ Why is direct speech better in 'Equal Rights'? How does the small amount of direct speech help 'The Visitor'?

▭▷ In pairs, say some short sentences to each other and then put them into reported speech, for example:

'I like chips.'
She said that she liked chips.

Put this part of 'Equal Rights' into reported speech: From 'Have you seen your dad yet.' to 'Don't be late . . .' Discuss any problems you had with either direct or reported speech.

*FOOTNOTE*

Note these things about reported speech:

1 You do not need speech marks as you are not putting down the *actual* words used. You are not quoting.
2 You report in the past time (past tense)
3 'I' becomes 'she' in the story 'Equal Rights'. If it was a boy it would be 'he'.
4 The word 'that' is often used to introduce reported speech:

She replied *that* she lived round the corner.

# YOU AND YOUR LIBRARY

15

How to use a library is one of the most important skills that you can learn at school. Once you know how to use it, you will have this skill for life to help you at work and play. Here we give you more guidance.
We also look at the skill of making notes from what you find in a library.

## Understanding a book's number

Imagine you have a new cycle and want to find a book with some general advice on cycling. If there is such a book in your library, it will almost certainly have the numbers 796.6 on its spine. Why has the subject 'cycling' been numbered 796.6? It has been given that number to help you find it.
Even in a small library there could be ten thousand non-fiction books on an enormous variety of subjects. To help

readers to find a book they have to be divided into groups or classes.
This simple exercise will help you understand the problem of doing this.

## Making groups

▭ All these words refer to people. Write them out in four groups. Give each group a heading.

German, nephew, doctor, baby, plumber, Brazilian, girl, grandmother, Indian, teacher, son, boy, Scot, busdriver, daughter, electrician, American, woman, father, man.

▭ Compare your groups and test how well your groups work by adding these words to the right one.

niece, parson, child, Australian

Each group is a class – a name by which we can refer to many words that have something in common.

What is the general word or class for each of these groups?

hammer, chisel, saw, screwdriver

hut, house, palace, school

daisy, daffodil, violet, rose, tulip, buttercup

cars, cycles, aeroplanes, gliders, motor-
bikes, ships, hovercraft

(Could this last group be divided up further?)

Did you have problems? In a library the problem is much greater because you are dealing with all the things humans know.

*FOOTNOTE*

A man called Dewey invented the groups (classes) that best tackled the problem. He first divided all non-fiction books into ten classes, each class had a number. These are his ten classes. Some of them may sound hard to understand – don't worry if you don't understand a word like 'philosophy'.

000 Generalities
100 Philosophy
200 Religion
300 Social Sciences
400 Languages
500 Pure Sciences
600 Technology
700 The Arts and Recreation
800 Literature
900 Geography and History

In small groups, discuss the following.

1 What kind of books might come under '200'?
2 What kind of books might come under '600'?
3 What kind of books might come under '800'?
4 What kind of books might come under '700'?
5 What kind of books might come under '900'?

Class 700 is 'The Arts and Recreation'. Cycling is a recreation so our book on cycling will be in the 700 class. Now look at the chart on page 108 to see how it gets the number 796.6 on its spine.

# How a subject gets its number

This chart shows you how the number for cycling is arrived at.

## STAGE 1

All knowledge is divided into 10:

### GENERAL CLASSES

000  General works
100  Philosophy
200  Religion
300  Social sciences
400  Language
500  Science
600  Technology
**700  Arts and Recreation** ⟶ is divided into 10 related topics all about arts and recreation
800  Literature
900  History and Geography

## STAGE 2

710  Town planning
720  Architecture
730  Sculpture
740  Drawing
750  Painting
760  Graphics
770  Photography
780  Music
**790  Recreation** ⟶ is divided into 10 related topics all about recreation

## STAGE 3

791  Public performances
792  Theatre
793  Indoor games
794  Games of skill
795  Games of chance
**796  Outdoor sports and games** ⟶ is divided into 10 related topics all about outdoor sport
797  Aquatic and air sports
798  Equestrian sports
799  Fishing and hunting and shooting

## STAGE 4

796.1  Miscellaneous e.g. kites, leapfrog
796.2  Games requiring equipment e.g. skateboarding, rollerskating
796.3  Ball games e.g. football, tennis
796.4  Athletics
796.5  Outdoor life e.g. walking, camping
**796.6  Cycling**
796.7  Racing cars and bikes
796.8  Combat sports e.g. boxing, karate

# Finding a non-fiction book

1 Find the Subject Index, a file box, where all the subjects are set out in alphabetical order. (Some libraries have this on computer.)

2 Supposing you wanted a book on *boa-constrictors*. It wouldn't be under 'B' – think of how large the subject index would be, if it had an entry for all animals under their separate names. It might well be under 'S' for snakes. You look under 'S' and find the subject number for snakes is 597.9.

3 Then you would go along the shelves of information books, find '500', then, using the numbers on the spines, eventually find 597.9.

4 Lastly you would have to use the index of any book on snakes to find boa-constrictors.

▭ Use the subject index of a library to do the following:

1 Find the subject numbers for these subjects in your index.

   cats
   houses
   poetry
   whales
   toys

2 See if you can find the subject number for these subjects by using another word which means the same.

   spooks
   funny books
   automobiles
   angling
   dress

3 See if you can find the subject number for these subjects. Use a broader term.

   owls
   netball
   breast stroke
   tabby
   killer whales

# Making notes

One of the most useful skills in English you can learn is to make proper *notes*. Notes are the few words we use to remind us of what we have read or heard. You should only aim to pick out the main things in notes.

You have to write a short piece, about 100 words, or give a one minute talk on the rings that appear mysteriously in cornfields. You find this article (page 111) in *Scoop* in your library.

You make these notes:

1 Spotted in Japan, Australia, France, Brazil and US but Southern England most
2 Over 400 reported in last few years
3 Some as big as 50 feet in diameter
4 Not just cornfields – mustard, beet, potatoes
5 No one has seen one being made
6 Professor Archibald Roy said 'I don't understand these circles'
7 Dr Terence Meaden is writing a book on it
8 Some scientists say not UFOs
9 Could be animals running in circles
10 Witchcraft
11 Whirlwinds most popular theory
12 Could be hoaxers
13 We may never know true answer

**REMEMBER: Notes are just a few words to remind you. They need not be sentences.**

▭ Decide which are the six most important notes. Put each of them on a card and then give a short talk – not more than a minute – to your group.

▭ Now write your article of not more than 100 words on 'The Riddle of the Rings'. You will now need to write in *sentences*. Be sure to write what you think is most important.

▭ Now go to your library and find a book or a magazine that has information or an article that interests you. Make notes on it. Then give a short talk to your group and write a short article.

# RIDDLE OF THE RINGS

PAUL MORRIS

**Here's a riddle you'll never work out! What's the connection between UFOs, whirlwinds, stampeding hedgehogs and human hoaxers? Give up?....*Scoop's* been investigating so read on...**

● Well, they are all possible explanations for the mysterious circles that suddenly appear in cornfields all over the world.

They've been spotted in Japan, Australia, France, Brazil and the United States, but it's southern England that has by far the most.

Over 400 have been reported just in the last few years and they range in size with some as big as 50 feet or more in diameter.

And they haven't just been in cornfields either – they've been spotted in crops of mustard, beet and even potatoes.

The reason there are so many theories flying around is because no one has ever seen one of these circles made.

It seems that one day the corn is standing thick and high – the next, as if by magic, huge swathes have been flattened – often in perfect circles.

### Human hoaxers out for a laugh?

And the experts seem to be as puzzled as we are! Professor Archibald Roy of Glasgow University has said: "I simply don't understand these circles. I'm totally convinced that it's a very – how shall I put it – a very interesting mystery. None of the explanations seem to fit."

Author Dr Terence Meaden is writing a book about the rings, but says,"I'm not making it public yet, because I have more work to do before I publish my results, but they link these phenomena into a bigger picture."

Of course, the theory we'd all like to believe is that the rings are in fact left after little green men have landed their UFOs for a few close encounters of the third kind.

But some scientists have poo-pooed this idea. They say UFOs could not be the cause because not all the circles are round and many of the flattened crops are layered – meaning whatever caused them was probably moving around.

This has led to other theories involving animals like hedgehogs and deer running round in circles in large packs. But this seems hard to believe and surely the animals would have been seen.

And because the rings differ so much in size and shape, whirling blades from helicopters are also doubtful.

There's even been a more controversial suggestion – that the rings are caused by witchcraft or druids.

And of course, whenever there's a mystery like this, there are doubters who say it's simply human hoaxers out for a laugh. But why anyone should want to do it they can't say – and how come they've never been caught after all these years?

### Whirlwind or UFO theory the winner?

So it would seem the most likely explanation is the weather. Most people believe the whirlwind theory is the winner.

They reckon a vicious, spiralling column of air moving over the fields may flatten the crops. But there's still a problem. Why should the circles differ so much in size, shape and groupings? And why should some be anti-clockwise and some clockwise?

At the end of the day you pays your money and you takes your choice. Who knows, we may never know the true answer – unless, of course, someone spots the little green men!

*111*

# MAKE YOUR OWN MAGAZINE

## 16

You've nearly reached the end of this book. Now we want you to bring all the skills you have learned to write your own magazine.

## A longer project

There are more than 6000 magazines published regularly in this country. Before you begin this project, look at some of these magazines. Look at the type of articles they contain and the design.

▭ Work in small groups (of 3–5). You will need to have a meeting first to decide certain things about your magazine.

1 Which group of people is your magazine for? (This might mean changes in your normal groups, so that you can find common interests.) The audience of your magazine could be:

A very young children
B girls or boys
C teenagers
D old people

E people with special interests – computers, games, walking, fishing, cooking, etc.

You might decide to try to interest people of all ages and interests, but this is difficult. It is easier to write for a specific audience. Remember that the language you use and the subjects you write about will vary with your readers.

2 The title – must be something to catch the interest and to give a good idea of what the magazine is about.

3 The material – will it have articles on famous or ordinary people. Will there be lots of photographs, drawings, cartoons? Will there be a letters page, a problem page? Will there be true stories or fictional ones?

4 How will you set out your magazine? Will you use colour? How much will your magazine cost?

5 Most magazines depend on advertisements to make them pay. You can have a few, but don't spend too long on this, and invent the product, don't use real ones.

On pages 114–123 are some magazine features for you to judge. Some are from real magazines, and some were written for magazines like your own by people your own age. These are the kinds of features you could have in your own magazine. With some of the features, there is work for you to do which would be part of your magazine or simply practice to help you decide which type of feature you are best at.

▭ Before you begin your magazine, each group should make a copy of this form and fill it in. It will help you to have a clearer idea of what you are doing, and help your teacher to see who has contributed what to the group project.

## Outline of project

(To be cleared by teacher before work starts.)

## Names of group members

Choose an editor, to make final decisions if there are any disputes.

## Audience for magazine

Age:
Interests:

## Ideas for contents

Idea:
Name of pupil:
(Each pupil must take responsibility for at least two contributions.)

## Format

Ideas for size of paper to be used, type, use and proportion of typed/word-processed pieces, etc.

## Possible sources of material

Library: which section? non-book materials?
People/institutions to write to.
People to interview.
People who could help and in what capacity.

# The comic

Comic illustrators are very skilled people. We do not expect you to be able to draw like this, though some of you may have ambitions. Try tracing a few of your favourite comic characters – you can learn from this.
The language in the bubbles does not always match the quality of the drawings. Take any page of a comic, this one for example, and put in your own words.

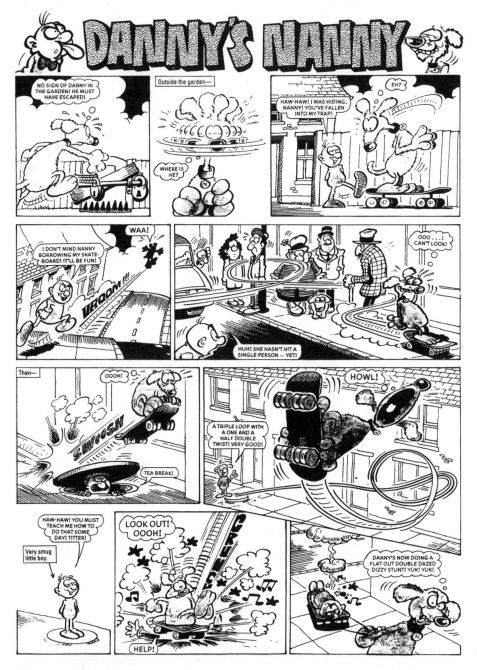

114

## An argument

Will you give your readers the opportunity to express their views? These two readers disagree. Write, in the form of a letter, either a contribution to the dog-watch debate or one expressing strong views on a subject of your own. It could be a national or a local matter. You might like to write on a 'green' issue.

### Dog watch

I AGREE with Moray council who are banning dogs from all the local parks. Many of Britain's parks are contaminated with a parasite spread by dogs' dirt. If a child is infected by this parasite it can cause blindness and other illnesses. I like dogs but I think they should be exercised where children don't play.

> Joy Wilkie, 12,
> from Dundee.

IT is, I think, an appalling decision by Moray council to ban dogs from all of their parks.

I appreciate the fact that dog faeces can spread disease, but so can a huge range of other animals, and also bi-products of varying description.

Is it then fair to ban just one source of possible infection, which can only affect individuals, rather than the population as a whole, unlike some other 'danger sources'.

I can, and so, take this one step further, and pose this question: Do we have the right, or even claim to have the right, to try and prevent any natural threat to our well being, whether it be dogs' droppings, or AIDS?

We have, as a race, adopted an unfortunate attitude in that we consider ourselves to be all important, superior to all other life forms on our planet, that we must survive, no matter what the cost.

I believe that we should leave our fate, as individuals and as a race entirely to nature, and not even attempt to cure diseases whatever their nature.

People all too easily forget the dogs and their owners. Well I remind you, Moray and your supporters, that others have rights too.

> Kevin Griffiths, 14,
> from Llanwrda, Dyfed.

Part I    New Story

# LOST

## ROMANCE

**At 5:40pm**

She banged her fingers on the till. The money drawer popped out, she pulled out a five pound note and handed it to the woman waiting for her change. She smiled at the woman and said "Thank you for shopping here, please come again."

She hated going through the same tedious procedure with each equally boring customer. She looked at the vacant sign in one of the windows and wondered who'd be the next victim for the dreaded cash till. She was sick and tired of working in a busy supermarket. Two weeks of her summer holidays had already passed. She needed the money to buy some fashionable clothes to wear in the sixth form.

"Excuse me" a voice interrupted her thoughts. She looked up into the greenest eyes she had ever seen. She stammered to say something. Finally her brain returned and offered some inspiration. She accepted and said "Yes can I help you."

"I hope you can, I've come about the vacancy" the tall dark boy said.

"Oh, um about the vacancy. You have to have an interview with the manager who is in his office. As you probably already know you don't need any qualifications for the job. You just have to pass the managers test." She answered him openly.

"Thanks, oh what's your name?"

"Janie, Janie Saunders."

"I'm Scott Kramer, it's great now that we know each other's names since I'm going to work here."

With that comment he walked off. Janie had never seen such an overconfident person before. She thought to herself i hope he gets the job work might even be "fun" with him around.

## NEXT MORNING

In the morning she felt sick so she rang the supermarket to tell them that she couldn't come in. A male voice answered the telephone she told him her message. Somehow the voice sounded familiar yes it was definitely familiar.

The voice returned and said "Hey, Janie its me Scott from the supermarket. Guess what? I got the job."

"That's good" scott, did you give my message." Janie said trying to hide the pleasure from her voice.

"Yes the boss says it's fine. i'll be seeing you then, here's my first customer."

"Bye." Continued on next page

23

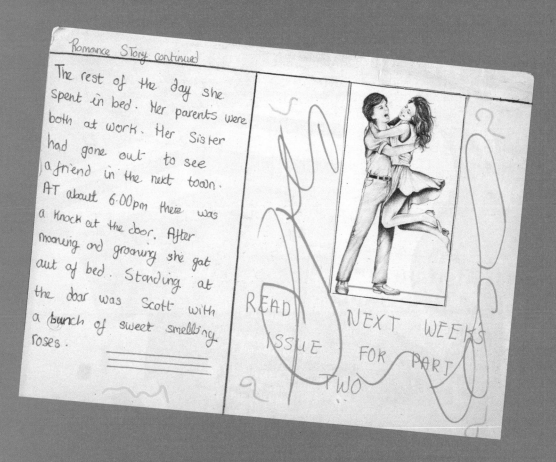

Romance Story continued

The rest of the day she spent in bed. Her parents were both at work. Her Sister had gone out to see a friend in the next town. AT about 6.00pm there was a knock at the door. After moaning and groaning she got out of bed. Standing at the door was Scott with a bunch of sweet smelling roses.

READ NEXT WEEK'S ISSUE FOR PART TWO

## A serial story

The most important feature of the serial story is that you must make your readers want to know what happens next – so that they buy the next issue. Remember cliff-hangers in the plays.

Here's an attempt, by someone of your own age, at an episode from a 'Romance' serial. Do you think she has caught the right style, content and presentation?

If you have decided to have a serial feature in your magazine, it could be any type of story – Ghost, Science Fiction, Detective, Adventure, for instance – that you think would interest your particular readership.

Perhaps you'd like to continue the story for a page, trying to catch the style Jane adopted.

## The unusual

Magazine readers always like to hear about the one in a million chance. Perhaps you know of an amazing occurrence. You could even make one up.

While you are doing your magazine, search for unusual stories in magazines and papers. You might like to put one of them in your magazine.

## Huntsman shot dead by his dog

**From CHRIS MOSEY in Stockholm**

AN elk hunter has met a bizarre death — shot by his own dog.

The accident happened near the small town of Vara, in central Sweden, where the hunter, Lars Carlsson, 48, ran a slaughterhouse.

On a weekend hunting trek into the forest Carlsson's long-haired dachshund, Tjabo, became involved in a fight with another dog.

Carlsson and his friend Lars-Erik Nilsson put down their rifles and pulled the two dogs apart.

Tjabo broke free and rushed towards his master, but in doing so ran over the rifles treading on the trigger of one of them.

As the gun went off Carlsson put out his hand to protect himself.

Instead he deflected the bullet through his heart and died instantly.

Inspector Lars-Hakan Ohlsson, local police chief who investigated the accident, said the safety catch on the rifle had become dislodged accidentally.

# A quiz

Are you a 'Mr Angry' or are you a 'calm and reasonable sort of person'. Do the 'Blowing Your Top' quiz and then try to invent one of your own.
Some suggestions:

Are you a Healthy Eater?
Are you a Good Son/Daughter?

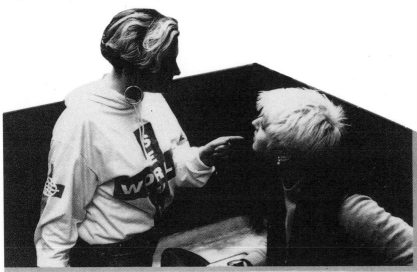

## BLOWING YOUR TOP: ARE YOU A MR ANGRY?!

*Are you a calm and reasonable sort of person or a total terror when you're angry? If you're not sure how you rate, try our quick quiz and see how far up the angry scale you get!*

**1. You stand for ages in a long queue waiting to pay for a jacket you really want. However, when it comes to your turn, the cashier stops serving and turns round to talk to one of her friends. What do you do?**

**a.** Stand there patiently until she stops talking, then go home and moan on to your mum about how rude she was.
**b.** Say "EXCUSE ME!" and then give her the jacket, and walk out with your head held high....you don't want the jacket *that* badly.
**c.** Have a complete tantrum, turn red, scream and demand to see the manager, then try to get the assistant fired.

**2. You want to watch a really sloppy film on TV but your brothers decide that they'd rather watch a James Bond movie. You were there first, but they take no notice of you. What do you do?**

**a.** Moan and groan as much as possible, and if they still don't budge, give up and go and do something else.
**b.** Scream and yell that it's not fair, and then cry and whinge till you get your way.
**c.** Give up and stay in your room in a huff and hope that they feel guilty.

**3. Your boyfriend lets you down at the last minute and it's not the first time. What do you do about it?**

**a.** Have a tantrum, chuck him and then go out with his best friend.
**b.** Nothing. After all, you're sure he couldn't help it!
**c.** Tell him that you aren't going to stand for it anymore, but feel guilty later and ring him up and apologise.

**4. You have arranged to go to the cinema with your best friend, but she turns up 45 minutes late and you miss the film. What do you do?**

**a.** Nothing. You're so mad you just sulk all evening.
**b.** Get really angry with her and tell her that if she's ever late again, you won't wait.
**c.** Rant and rave at her, then stomp off and wait for her to come round and apologise.

**5. Your mum promises to wash your jeans so that you can wear them to a party on Friday night. But come Friday night, they are still in the wash basket. What do you do?**

**a.** Rant 'n' rage, tell your mum she's ruined your life and refuse to accept her apology.
**b.** Wear something else, it's not the end of the world.
**c.** Wear the dirty jeans and hope that your mum feels guilty.

### HOW YOU SCORED

1. a-0  b-5  c-10
2. a-5  b-10 c-0
3. a-10 b-0  c-5
4. a-0  b-5  c-10
5. a-10 b-5  c-0

### THOSE RANTING RESULTS

**0-10** Well, you certainly let people walk all over you don't you? OK! So you don't like confrontations or arguments, but then you secretly hate being taken for a ride as well. You know, there's nothing wrong with a bit of anger now and then, it can be good for you and it's miles better than bottling up all your feelings then exploding in private. If you start putting your foot down now and again, people will stop taking you for granted.

**15-30** You've got the balance just right. You know when to get angry and when not to. You don't bottle things up and you believe in saying what and when things annoy you. If you find yourself guilty of having a tantrum now and then, don't worry, it's perfectly natural — no-one's perfect!

**35-50** Do you ever notice how people run for cover whenever you get angry? Well, it's hardly surprising is it? You let your anger get totally out of hand and then lash out at any poor unsuspecting person who happens to be around. If you don't want to be known as Mr Angry for the rest of your life, you'd better calm down and learn to reason instead of shouting.

## EIGHT THINGS TO DO WHEN YOU FEEL LIKE YOU'RE GOING TO EXPLODE

**1.** Physical exertion is a great anger release! Try going for a run or put on your favourite record really loud and dance round your room till you have no energy left. Any game which involves hitting is also good, as is housework such as tidying your bedroom or scrubbing the kitchen floor.

**2.** Write down exactly why you are angry and exactly how you feel. Then when you've got it all out of your system, rip up the letter. You'll be surprised at how much better you'll feel.

**3.** Taking a long walk is a very good way to work out your anger. Not only are you doing something physical, but you're also giving yourself time to think.

**4.** If you still feel angry, lock yourself in your room and punch your pillow and scream to your heart's content (it's advisable to put some loud music on before you do this). At least this way you won't be venting that angry energy on anything but your pillow.

**5.** Why not have a jolly good bawl?! Crying can be very therapeutic and is a great way to release all those pent-up feelings.

**6.** Count to ten. Corny as it may sound, this method does work. It won't of course prevent you from thinking angrily, but it will control your anger, long enough to stop you lashing out and making things worse.

**7.** Think really hard about the consequences your fury might have....it can be a very sobering thought and might stop you doing something rash.

**8.** Confront the person who's made you angry — but in a reasonable manner. It's no good screaming and shouting, take things slowly and calmly, and explain exactly to the person who's made you angry, why they have made you feel that way.

● The most important thing to remember about anger is that it is harmful to sit and simmer with your anger without expressing it in some way. Unexpressed anger does not go away, but tends to build up until you feel so miserable that you don't know what to do. Learning to work through your anger will not only relieve the people around you, but it will make you happier as well.

19

## Scared of school

**Please help. I am ten and will be changing school in a year's time and I'm so scared. Please print this letter.**
**Worried Bros fan.**

It is a bit frightening when you change from primary school to secondary school. It takes a bit of getting used to. So it's not surprising that you're feeling scared. Most people do. But you're starting to worry a bit early aren't you? You've got another year to go yet, and I'm pretty sure that you'll find that these fears will get a little bit less as that year goes on and you get that little bit older. Also, before you go, you'll have the chance to have a look round the schools in your areas. When you've chosen one and you've got a place, then you'll have another chance to go over and meet some of the staff. Some of the children in your present class are almost certainly going to be going to go to the same school as you, so the chances are that you won't have to face the challenge alone. So don't let yourself get into a state about it. OK?

## The problem page

Would you agree with the reply to this letter?
Write a comforting reply based on your own experience – or, if you think the writer is right to be worried, say how you have tried to overcome any problems you have had.

## The feature article

The feature article is always a popular part of a magazine. The one opposite tells us about the make-up of the body in an interesting way. Study how it's done and try to interest people about something you know – you might need to use the library – in a similar kind of article. It could be about a hobby, or a famous person, or a place of particular interest in your area. Remember, you are the expert. Try to catch the interest of people who know nothing or little about the subject.

# Slugs and Snails

## by Pete Rowan

SLUGS and snails and puppydogs' tails,
That's what little boys are made of.

There are all sorts of ways of looking at what the human body is made of. Before some rather off-beat ones, this is a scientific breakdown of the body of a grown-up weighing 65 kg:

| | | |
|---|---|---|
| Protein | 11 kg | 17% |
| Carbohydrate | 1 kg | 1.5% |
| Fat | 9 kg | 14% |
| Water | 40 kg | 61.5% |
| Minerals | 4 kg | 6.0% |

It can vary a great deal. A lot of people are overweight and their fat can rise to form 70 per cent of the body weight.

Now for some fun with these figures. Many of them have appeared in books before. They come originally from a politician called Sir W Grenfell. Others I've made up.

As you can see from the above your teacher has 40 kg of water in him or her. This is 40 litres – about enough to have a bath in. Water is made up of oxygen and hydrogen – H20 – and so there is enough hydrogen in your teacher to fill a balloon which could lift your mum to the top of Nelson's Column.

Blood and cucumbers are both around 99 per cent water. This makes them very similar.

Your dad has 5–6 litres of blood in him. This is equivalent to around ten cucumbers.

Now the fat in the body. In a normal person there's enough – if you wanted some for your 40-litre bath – to make seven bars of soap.

Part of the carbohydrate section (1 kg) is sugar. There's enough of this to fill a jam jar.

Now the skeleton. Your teacher's skeleton isn't made up of the sorts of old dry bones you see in museums and graveyards. They weigh about 9 kg. This is made up as follows:

| | |
|---|---|
| Protein | 1.8 kg |
| Water | 2.25 kg |
| Minerals | 4.50 kg |

The skeleton contains 99 per cent of the body's calcium – about 1.2 kg. From this you could make enough whitewash to paint a chicken coop. (Whitewash is a mixture of lime and water. Lime is calcium oxide).

The mineral section of the body is the one you can have most fun with. If your chicken coop needed some repair the human body has enough iron to make a medium (about 6 cm long) nail.

Sulphur is present in the body. Most is bound up in two amino acids. These are the building blocks of the body. Protein – needed for growth – is made up of strings of them. Anyway, there is enough sulphur in them to kill all the fleas on a dog.

The phosphorus – mainly in bones as phosphate – could make 2,200 match heads. The body's potassium – mostly inside cell water – could explode a toy cannon.

Finally a couple of questions. The body has about 2g of zinc. Zinc is used – among other things – in TV screens. How many standard (24″) TV screens are there in an average fully-grown teacher?

And, secondly, if your mum has all this hydrogen in her – why doesn't she float off?

# The book review

Discuss whether this review makes you want to read the book.
Write a book review of your own. It can be any kind of book, not necessarily fiction. Or it could be about the first part of the serial 'Romance' in this section.

---

```
Title:     The Cool Boffin
Author:    Pete Johnson
Publisher: Collins
```

## About the book

Richard Hodgson is a fat, spotty, bespectacled fifteen year-old boy – a typical boffin. He swots and swots while the world passes by in a blur. Richard is desperately trying to escape his boffin image. One day something happens that changes all of this. Richard – the world's number one boffin – becomes Ricky – cool, trendy and a bit of a rebel.

This book tells of Richard's dramatic turn-around and how he becomes pals with Steve Almond, someone all the girls fancy like crazy. He becomes a bit of a lad, holding wild parties and drinking. Richard's school work starts to suffer and the teachers notice a change, but he couldn't care less, or could he? Somehow things don't seem to be working out quite as he expected.

## What I thought about the story

This story was quite funny and witty in parts. It was easy to follow and read. I don't think it was very realistic because I couldn't really see someone changing so drastically in real life like Richard did. I enjoyed this book even though it wasn't very convincing in some parts. I think people who are shy and want to be noticed more might be able to relate easily with this story.

                                        Annabel Ellis

## Get your story

Newspapers nowadays have little news to report; they are always a day
behind TV and radio. So they need to look for more information on stories
already broadcast.
Here are two short items from radio news bulletins, though they weren't
broadcast in this way and the names and places have been changed.

Twenty-year-old Alan Geeson escaped with only a broken collar-bone and
wrist after he had woken up to find himself in a waste-collection vehicle on the
way to the crusher. He admitted being very drunk and climbing into a waste-
paper skip and falling asleep. 'I was sure I was going to die,' he said. I was
covered in waste of all kinds and, despite my banging and cries for help, the
driver didn't hear me even when he stopped to add other skipsfull of waste to
his load.'

A woman caused a two-mile traffic tailback which clogged up Brinsfield
yesterday when she accused a stallholder of selling her rotten tomatoes. She
took off her shoe and hit Mrs Betty Foreman on the head with it. A large crowd
gathered to watch the altercation which had the effect of stopping the traffic in
the town centre. Mrs Foreman suffered injuries to her head and an ambulance
had to be called.

▭ Role play in groups of four. Each member of the group should take one
of these parts:

Alan Geeson          Mrs Betty Foreman
The truck driver     The angry woman

Spend ten to fifteen minutes preparing your part, inventing details about
yourself and the incident. Each pair then should take turns to be reporters,
questioning the other two about their story. Make notes and take quotes.

▭ In pairs, make a newspaper report of your story. You have quotations
from the main characters involved. You will be able to add to the radio
stories. You might make up quotations from other people as well. For
instance, the real newspaper 'skip' story included quotations from a police-
spokesman and the manager of the waste-disposal firm – both were asked
why they didn't check skips to see if anyone was in them. What sort of
replies might they have given?
Set out your story in an eye-catching way and write a good headline.

# Language words

A list of words and terms to do with language follows. Go through them and consult with your teacher about any you are not sure of or have forgotten. The number after the words refers to where they are first mentioned in this book.

audience (page 8)

punctuation (14)

salutation (14)

subscription (14)

paragraph (14)

narrator (14)

summary (18)

capitals (18)

italics (18)

sub-headings (18)

exclamation marks (23)

speech bubble (23)

instructions (23)

key points (26)

alphabetical order (28)

define/definition (28)

parts of speech (28)

prefixes (30)

suffixes (30)

verbs (32)

pronouns (32)

nouns (32)

adjectives (32)

sentences (34)

myths (37)

legends (37)

direct speech (47)

inverted commas (47)

reported speech (47)

past tense (47)

present tense (50)

future tense (50)

statements (54)

questions (54)

exclamations (54)

Standard English (60)

Received Pronunciation (61)

subject (61)

plural (61)

singular (61)

dialogue (66)

argument (73)

narrative (82)

simile (86)

cliché (87)

advertising copy (92)

plot (96)

notes (110)

# Acknowledgements

We are grateful to the following for permission to reproduce copyright material:
the author's agent for the extract 'Tom Tit Tot' in *Akenfield* by Ronald Blythe
(Penguin Books Ltd, 1972); Jonathan Cape Ltd for an article by Pete Rowan,
originally published in *Early Times* 27.7.89; the author, Kevin Griffiths for his letter
in *Early Times* 24.8.89; the author, Orlando Patterson for his story 'The Visitor'; G A
Shapiro, on behalf of the author, for the article 'Cracking Down on Smacking' by
Jonathan Shapiro in *Early Times* 24.8.89; Solo Syndication & Literary Agency Ltd
for the article 'Huntsman shot dead by his Dog' by Chris Mosey in *Daily Mail*
24.10.89; Unwin Hyman Ltd for the story 'Equal Rights' by Bernard Ashley in
*Openings* by Roy Blatchford; the author, Joy Wilkie for her letter in *Early Times*
24.8.89.

We have been unable to trace the copyright holder in the letter and answer 'Scared
of School' in *Girl* magazine 2.8.89 and would appreciate any information that would
enable us to do so.

We are grateful to the following for permission to reproduce photographs and
other copyright material;
Allsport UK, page 52 (photo Vandystadt); J Allan Cash Photolibrary, pages 88 and
89; County Road Safety Officers Association, pages 24–5; Dominic Photography,
pages 64 and 65 below (photos Zoe Dominic), 65 centre (photo Catherine Ashmore);
Dover Publications Inc, 1970 and Harper & Bros New York, 1878, Gustav Doré, *The
Rime of the Ancient Mariner*, page 85; Dunlop Slazenger Golf Division, page 92;
EMAP/Metro Publications, *Just Seventeen*, page 119; Mary Evans Picture Library
(J.H. Fold in Lang's Blue Fairy Book), page 59; Finn Crisp, page 93 above; Ronald
Grant Archive, page 67; Sally and Richard Greenhill, page 76; *The Independent*,
pages 94 above (photo Jonathon Weaver), 94 below (photo Glynn Griffiths);
International Wool Secretariat, page 93 below; Sivkka-Liisa Konttineu, *Step by
Step*, Bloodaxe Books/Amber/Side, 1989, page 95; Mirror Group Newspapers/
Syndication International, *Daily Mirror* (photos by Ross Kinnaird/Empics), page 46;
Royal Pharmaceutical Society of Great Britain, pages 19–20; Planagraphic Printers,
*Scoop* (photo Paul Morris), page 111; Solo Syndication, *Daily Mail*, page 47; Theatre
am Turn, Frankfurt (photo Christa Dorner), page 65 above; D.C. Thomson, *Star
Love Stories in Pictures no. 1199 – Promised to Another*, 1989, page 23, *Annabel*,
August 1989, page 31 and *The Beano*, August 1989, page 114; G.K. Ward, page 109.
Photographs on pages 72, 80 and 101 were taken by John Birdsall.

Picture Research: Marilyn Rawlings

Illustrated by: Edward Mclachlan, pages 2/3, 33, 35, 68, Jessica Perry pages 9 and
11, Denyse Stephen pages 40 and 43.

Designed by Jenny Portlock of Pentaprism

LONGMAN GROUP UK LIMITED,
*Longman House, Burnt Mill, Harlow,*
*Essex CM20 2JE, England*
*and Associated Companies throughout the world.*

First published 1990

ISBN 0 582 05518 0

Set in 10½/12½ pt Versailles

Printed in Great Britain by
BPCC Hazell Books, Aylesbury